MRS. BEATON'S QUESTION

MY NINE YEARS AT THE HALIFAX SCHOOL FOR THE BLIND

by **ROBERT MERCER**

MRS. BEATON'S QUESTION

MY NINE YEARS AT THE HALIFAX SCHOOL FOR THE BLIND

by **ROBERT MERCER**

The Acorn Press
Charlottetown
2019

AC◯RNPRESS

P.O. Box 22024
Charlottetown, Prince Edward Island
C1A 9J2
acornpresscanada.com

Edited by Ann Thurlow
Cover illustration and design by Matt Reid
Printed in Canada

Library and Archives Canada Cataloguing in Publication

Title: Mrs. Beaton's question : my nine years at the Halifax School for the Blind / by Robert Mercer.
Names: Mercer, Robert, 1948- author.
Identifiers: Canadiana (print) 20190170913 | Canadiana (ebook) 20190171103 | ISBN 9781773660349 (softcover) | ISBN 9781773660356 (HTML)
Subjects: LCSH: Mercer, Robert, 1948- | LCSH: Halifax School for the Blind—Biography. | LCSH: Blind students—Nova Scotia—Halifax—Biography. | LCGFT: Autobiographies.
Classification: LCC HV1624.M47 A3 2019 | DDC 305.9/081092—dc23

Canada Council for the Arts   Conseil des Arts du Canada

The publisher acknowledges the support of the Government of Canada, the Canada Council of the Arts and The Province of Prince Edward Island.

I dedicate this book to my family from Sydney, Nova Scotia: parents Earle and Lillian Mercer (deceased); brothers Earl and Brian, and sisters Lillian Yhard, Eva Dicks, Gwen Leblanc, Shirley Matthews, Inez MacLennan, and Darlene Cuff. I've never been home without feeling welcome, no matter how long I've been away.

AUTHOR'S PREFACE

Why I ended up at the School for the Blind in Halifax and what it was like when I lived there from 1958 to 1967: that's what the book is about. It's not a detailed history, a gripping novel or a disapproving rant; it's the memories of one boy, lost for a time, and the school that found him.

Because I lived on the boys' side at the School, the book is mostly tilted in that direction. I'm quite sure, however, that what's written in these pages is pretty well what the girls would have said and probably said better. One voice or another, we were all the beneficiaries of a school with a proud history of accomplishment in the field of education, vocational training, and advocacy on behalf of the blind.

The School for the Blind in Halifax, formerly the Asylum for the Blind, was the first residential school of its kind in Canada, opening its doors to four students and two teachers in 1871. By the 1920s, annual enrolment had soared to 120 pupils, a testament to need, centuries of neglect, and the foresight of those who laid the foundation for what became one of the most highly regarded schools for the blind in North America and abroad.

It started with a generous donation of $5,000 and a large parcel of land in downtown Halifax from a wealthy merchant, William M. Murdock. Charles Frederick Fraser, later to be knighted for his years of service to the blind, was the first School Superintendent, a post he would occupy for all of fifty years.

Sir Frederick was himself totally blind and probably the first blind person from anywhere in Atlantic Canada to receive a formal education, and that, thankfully, from the world-renowned Perkins Institute for the Blind in Boston. The proven practices of the school in Boston provided a sound foundation for the new school in Halifax.

By the turn of the century, the School offered studies in reading, mathematics, history, piano tuning, massage, organ and piano, broom making, chair caning, gymnastics, crafts, and mobility training. The focus of studies, as Sir Frederick insisted, was on sound academic training and skills for later employment, a legacy that lasted throughout the life of the School.

As they did at the Perkins School in Boston, Sir Frederick gave preference to hiring blind teachers to work alongside those with sight, thereby providing successful role models for students and their families. For me and thousands of other students at the School, seeing firsthand what blind people could accomplish, whether as teachers, administrators, musicians, or support staff, was one of the most meaningful aspects of the old School.

Sir Frederick was a skilful, passionate leader and lobbyist, and under his direction the School flourished with more classrooms and residence space, innovative teaching methods, community outreach initiatives, and programs for the prevention of blindness.

Apart from its role in the field of educating blind children and adults, the School established the first circulating library of raised print and Braille books in Canada, and lobbied successfully for free postage of material for the blind, a privilege still afforded to this day. The School was also a leader in the development of advanced methods for doing mathematics in Braille.

Sir Frederick was instrumental in supporting the establishment of the Canadian National institute for the Blind and a number of self-help organizations of blind people aimed at advancing their own cause for employment opportunities and social gathering. And when called upon in 1917, the School, with help from the Perkins Institute and the American Red Cross, opened its doors to almost 200 men, women, and children who were blinded in the Halifax Explosion.

By the time the wrecking ball had taken down the old School in 1984, literally thousands of blind students from all four Atlantic Provinces, and a few from Quebec and the Caribbean, had passed through its doors. For most of them, it was a life-altering journey toward self-reliance, away from dependency at home, from the streets, the poorhouse, and hidden rooms.

For every story told in these pages, there's more to tell and other blind students to tell them, but not for much longer. I thought of that as I worked on the book. I thought of the dedicated teachers and other staff who worked there and the kids I lived with during my nine years in residence.

I kept thinking, as well, how fortunate we were that our residential school was not like the ill-fated schools for Aboriginal children. I could face being away from home, but I couldn't imagine having to face what some of them, regretfully, experienced.

Of course, not every blind student will see the School or what it did for them in exactly the same way as I describe it in these pages. Why? Because it's personal, life at the school as I saw it: two eyes upon the world, one entirely blind and the other not much better.

CHAPTER ONE

I was three or four years old before even knowing that I couldn't see very well. My eyes were noticeably scrambled up but I didn't know it. I couldn't see them in the mirror and didn't think to take a closer look until neighbours and strangers did, always asking me questions about my eyes and making comments afterwards. It was like nothing was wrong until everyone kept saying so.

"What's wrong with your eyes" was a kind of "hello" and, although I didn't know the answer, I figured out before long that something was wrong. The people who asked meant no harm, of course, and I didn't mind the attention, or the nickels either. But questions like that were usually followed with whispers of "poor Robert" or "how sad," like being nearly blind meant I couldn't hear what they were saying. Every time they pitied me in that way, I felt less than them and smaller than before.

I was happy the way I was, before the comments, and I would have sprouted wings or given away my favourite toy for a simple, "Well, Robert, aren't you doing well!" or words to that effect.

No one bothered me like that at home or talked to me like I was the new baby in the crib that year. I saw what I saw and the very idea that there was more out there to see, images and clarity beyond what I saw, made no sense to me. I believed it, though, as unbelievable as it all sounded.

Poor eyesight aside, I was a little boy at heart, a magnet for adventure and mischief, as was Earl, my younger brother by one year. Earl and I were inseparable back then. It was seldom "Robert did it" or "Earl did it"; it was mostly "Robert and Earl did it." We shared the fun, and when we were bad we took the blame. To quote Dad, we were "two little Christers." "Do that again," he'd say, "and I'll crucify the both of you!" A few spankings over the years, and a lot of loud barking, but Dad was a good man who cared about all of us in his own untalkative way.

We lived on Townsend Street in Sydney, Nova Scotia, just up the way from the train tracks, near a brook, a bakery, and a lumberyard. Practically next door was Sid's Pool Hall, the Steel City Tavern, and Kay's Cozy

Corner restaurant: still there today and still making hamburgers. Altogether, it was an interesting and lively place to grow up.

That was my home and back yard for a while and, when there, my parents left me free to run and play, to fall down and get up by myself. I fell down more than Earl and the other kids but seldom twice in the same place.

I attended St. Joseph's School at the age of six and for that year and the two that followed, I hardly remember even walking either to or from school, let alone what happened there. But I do recall being told, each year, to move my desk up close, nearer the blackboard, in front of all the other kids. I remember how it felt, sitting nose to nose with chalk marks I couldn't read, always in the teacher's way while the other kids looked on, teasing and whispering.

I'm sure now that some of the whispering and teasing was just in my head, but still, it set me apart from the other kids at school. I felt alone and, from that, I learned to be painfully shy and withdrawn. The classroom was certainly not like home and the school playground was not my back yard either. By then, long before the world had embraced diversity, or said it did, I was well aware of being different.

I won a prize in Grade One for being the "quietest" boy in the class. It was a picture of the Blessed Virgin

Mary, framed in ornate, see-through plastic. It felt good inside to win something, and I was proud to bring it home, but Virgin Mary or not, it was no blessing to be that quiet all the time.

Still, I managed to pass Grade Primary and Grades One and Two and always with gold and silver stars on my report card: the ones that sparkled to say how well I had done that year.

CHAPTER TWO

I was eight and headed for Grade Three in 1957 when Mom and Dad bought a house for $850 and moved us—six children and one on the way—from the busy paved streets of Sydney to a dusty dirt road in the country. It was our "new" home, a fifty-year-old, two-storey hay barn, partly made over and just about what you'd expect for $850.

We had running water, heat, electricity, an outhouse, a kitchen, a living room, and three slanted-roof bedrooms upstairs: one for Mom, Dad, and the newest baby that year; one for the four girls; and a third bedroom for the two little Christers. It got even more crowded upstairs when babies eight and nine arrived.

Some of the walls in the house were papered in newsprint and even I could see the outside through the cracks. There were little snakes under the floorboards, a forest in the back yard, a farm up the road, and lakes all around for swimming and fishing. For Earl and me, it was free range, one big back yard to explore and conquer. The forest was ours to forage and, no matter the season, it became our second home.

Each year, in the Catholic way, a new sibling was added to the family and, before long, there were nine of us, a baseball team. My two older sisters, Lillian and Eva, arrived first, in that order, with me next and then Earl, Gwennie, Shirley, Inez, Brian, and Darlene.

Sisters Gwen and Shirley were old enough to enjoy the open space and fresh air of the country. Lillian, being all of thirteen, probably thought she was being punished for something she hadn't done, and Eva: she never talks about the house or antics in the country without a good laugh, and Lillian likewise.

It wasn't long before Dad converted the hay barn into a proper home with new and used everything from the basement up. The outhouse gave way to a chemical toilet and then a real one later on. There was always work to be done and we all pitched in.

We laugh about the day Mom cooked supper for the Queen who was scheduled to pass by our house one afternoon. "What if her car breaks down," Mom would defend herself, "I can't not offer her a bite to eat." Or the day Earl tripped down the stairs with the chemical toilet, and Mom trying to sweep it up as the insurance man was ambling up the lane to collect his twenty-five-cent monthly premium.

If there wasn't a pile of wood for Earl and me to saw and chop, there was coal to shovel into the basement or earth to sieve for the garden. I used the saw, the sledgehammer, the little axe, and the big one. I was told to be careful more times than needed but, apart from that, it was full steam ahead.

We all worked at something and, before long, we got to like the house that Dad built—with everyone's help and all kinds of stuff left over at the steel plant where he worked. We weren't the Waltons, for sure, but we had our share of fun in those days and in that old house; memories of it are rerun like movies whenever the family gathers.

The move to the country, however, didn't do much for my self-esteem. The teasing at the new school, St. Augustine, was no less hurtful than at the old one. On a typical walk to school, some of the kids couldn't let me by without name-calling. I found the days in school to be longer than weeks, and the blackboard just as blurry as the one at St. Joseph's. The only thing worse for me than time in the classroom was recess on the playground.

I could see well enough for some of the games—most of them played by the girls, like skipping rope and hopscotch. But I was too shy to play with the girls and too slow and awkward for the boys. Instead, I watched and cringed whenever anyone came near. There were times when the teacher would make me join in, a pigeon among the cats, and that was worse still.

It was hard for kids not to notice that the iris in both my eyes was deformed and the pupils off-centre. What they didn't see were the more serious problems hidden well inside and behind the eyes. It was called Coloboma, a defect in prenatal growth of one or more parts of the eye. There was some talk of an operation, just after birth, but it was too risky for what little good it might have done. Fortunately, my parents chose instead to leave well enough alone and take me home as I was.

In any case, the damage was widespread, affecting the irises, the pupils, both lenses, both retinas, and, not to be left out, the optic nerve, the all-important transmitter. Thankfully, my brain learned at an early age, and all by itself, to fill in the gaps and see beyond the blurry pictures.

And maybe that's why I could see well enough as a child to read print close-up with the good eye and colours well enough to stay inside the lines. I could see faces—but without features; not much of anything across the street; and less still when facing the sun.

And if that wasn't enough to draw attention, I walked to school with my head down because I could see better that way, shielded from the sun and nearer the ground. And that silly "sticks-and-stones" rhyme about names never hurting: don't believe it.

I didn't know, back then, but I was my own worst enemy, too shy and tentative, too timid and afraid of my own shadow. It was like everyone at school was looking at me, all the time. I didn't see them do it but the thought of it was in my head, as real as it gets.

In hindsight, I might have coped a lot better if I wasn't so bothered about what the other kids thought, or at least what I thought they were thinking. If only I'd had the nerve, back in the day, to speak up and stand up for myself. It shouldn't have been that difficult but, simply speaking, it just wasn't me.

My parents might have seen lower marks on term report cards that year, but nothing was ever written about the more serious problems on the playground. They saw me as I was at home, not the way I was at school. And even then, what could they have done? There was no extra help at local schools for those who couldn't see the blackboard and no arms outstretched to guide their parents either.

In the case of my parents, no one came to the rescue, at least not at first. They did their best, which should have been enough, but it wasn't. I doubt if anyone tried to help them at the hospital when I was born. I can only imagine what it was like for them when the nurse came in with the newborn followed by the doctor with the bad news. What a worrisome, stressful day that must have been, full of sadness, confusion, grief, and probably fear of what was to come.

CHAPTER THREE

The terms blindness and visual impairment are often coupled as one, and although total blindness is vastly more challenging than the other, the impact of each is different only by degrees. I was visually impaired and not that far from blindness, and not just because I failed the big "E" test in the doctor's office. It was more that in my good eye, the world was always blurry, and in the bad one, there was nothing but dim light and shadows.

What little light and shadows remained in my bad eye, the left one, soon disappeared when the better eye took centre stage and closed the curtain on the other. They called it a "lazy" eye. Not having to perform, it gave up and stopped looking by the time I was twelve or thirteen. The readings on the doctor's eye chart came out exactly the same as before, like nothing at all had changed. But for me, it was a big loss. While it was alive and enlightened, my left eye was always on alert for shadows that told me when to turn my head for a closer look. Gone were the light and the blurred shadows on my left side, and, with them, a little balance and a lot of perspective. The world afterwards was mostly right-sided and straight ahead.

I was fortunate, though, to see anything at all, considering the extent of damage, especially to the optic nerve. But frankly, being lucky on that front, whether at my old school in Sydney or now in the country, didn't count for much when I was young and just trying to fit in.

I hardly spoke to anyone at school and hardly anyone spoke to me. I'm tempted to say "so what" as I write, but at the time, and just like today, making friends and fitting in was everything. And there I was, on stage in the wrong play, lagging behind and not very happy about it.

I can see clearly now that the daytime nightmares at school were more of my own making than just kids being kids. Why I was so self-conscious, timid, and afraid, I'm not sure, but that, too, probably had something to do with poor eyesight. When you don't see well enough to be sure of much, you take tiny steps and sometimes none at all. It's part of the package, or at least it was part of what got delivered to me. Back then, I just wanted to sit in the same rows as the other kids. I probably wanted to see like them as well.

All that to say, Grade Three was not a good year at the new school in the country. But, eventually, as tides and time stop for no boy, the year came to an end and, finally, it was Grading Day.

Grading Day was my favourite time of the year, partly that school was over but mostly because I'd always made the grade. It was the day that someone told the whole world that "poor Robert" had done well that year, and that's all I needed for a good summer.

I arrived home on Grading Day with the sealed envelope and gave it to Mom. She scanned the first three folds of the report card (no stars) and read the last line first:

"Robert is *not* recommended for advancement to Grade Four." *Wait, what?* I thought to myself.

"It's nothing to worry about, Robert," Mom was quick to point out. "It's good to be held back sometimes. You'll do better next year, you'll see." See or not, I was gravely wounded, ashamed, and embarrassed. No one else failed Grade Three, or no one I knew.

It wasn't the idea of repeating the grade that bothered me. It was more that I had failed and everyone would know it; more reason to look. What would it say to the whisperers or the kids who called me "crosseyed monkey"? I didn't cry about it outwardly, but inside I felt strangely ill.

As close as we all were at home, I told no one how it felt, not even my brother, Earl. Besides, what would I have said? The bad feeling was all over me and how does a nine-year-old explain that? Ours was a close family but we were much better at laughing and arguing than spilling out the deeper stuff.

By noon that day I had gotten over some of the bad news and was outside, in the back yard, lamenting the rest, when a red dress turned smartly into the driveway. It was my teacher, Mrs. Flynn. *What's she doing here*, I wondered. *Maybe she made a mistake and came to fix it or maybe she just changed her mind.*

I hurriedly went into the house and upstairs without being seen. I lay down with an ear to the floor and I listened, waiting for the good news.

"Mrs. Mercer," Mrs. Flynn began, "Robert tries hard to keep up at school but he's falling behind, more and more every day. How he ever got to Grade Three, I don't know." *What does she mean, she doesn't know*, I thought? *Did I fail those grades, too?*

"It's not Robert's fault," she continued, "but with forty kids in the classroom, I've no extra time to help him. There's a school in Halifax that teaches blind children like Robert and I think you should..."

"I'm sorry, dear," Mom interrupted, "I can't send Robert that far from home. He's only nine!" By the time the tears had dried and Mrs. Flynn had left the house, two things were clear. First, I wasn't expelled from school, but, secondly, I wasn't allowed to go back there either. Mrs. Flynn was clear on that point.

In those days, before people knew better, local schools were not equipped to educate blind children, and, in fairness to them, they were not funded to do so either. But in Halifax, two hundred and fifty miles away, there was a school for blind children, funded in part by the four Atlantic provinces and the rest from private donations.

Anyway, I didn't have to go there or back to the school up the street either. I couldn't believe my ears, or at least the one on the floor. For a time I was on cloud nine, living my happiest moment ever. *Imagine*, I thought, *no school, ever again!* It got me back to feeling better.

I thought more favourably about Mrs. Flynn that afternoon, but, of course, for all the wrong reasons. Today, as I see it much better, she deserves all the gold stars left in the universe. She was a brave teacher, the first to tell it as it was, the way someone had to tell it, sooner or later.

CHAPTER FOUR

There was always a place for me at home and, most times, unlike in the classroom, I sat pretty well where I liked. Mom might tell Earl, though younger, to take care of me when off we'd go on a fishing trip, but that was just Mom being motherly. I lost battles at home and I won some, too, but I battled like everyone else and that's what mattered.

Eva would read us fairy tales and she and Lillian would help me with my homework. I spent time as well with Gwennie who, by then, was seven and good at everything that matters when you're seven: puzzles, board games, hopscotch, and skipping rope.

Over the years, Gwennie, Eva, Earl and I picked blueberries enough for a thousand pies. Eva might have seen white and green ones in my blueberry pail, but I'm sure they were blue when I picked them.

There was no weekly allowance at home so we learned to make our own way in whatever way there was. We sold kindling, minnows, worms, bottles, bunnies we raised, scrap metal, and blueberries door to door. There was always something to get into and although I was a bit slower at it, I got it done and no one ever complained.

As much as I liked to be at home, it was stressful at times because Mom suffered from manic depression or bipolar disorder, as it's now called. Mom called it "bad nerves," and, somehow, through it all, she took care of us, feeding and clothing nine children—and half the kids in the neighbourhood. The family took care of her as well, whether she was depressed for a month or manically annoying for a day.

For Mom it was fourteen loaves of bread, baked twice a week; meals from soup bones and whatever was on sale or in-season at the grocery store. For dessert it was pies and sweets made from free blueberries or spotted fruit from the local grocer, just before closing on Friday afternoons. It was ten cents for a huge bag that Lillian and Eva could barely carry. If there was an angle to make a dollar into two, Mom knew all about it.

When she was sick, which was often and sometimes long-term, the girls mostly took care of the house while Dad, Earl, and, later on, Brian, did the heavy lifting. As the years passed, all the kids, right down to Darlene, would be called upon to lend a helping hand. I did my part, too, for a time and would have done more if not for what happened later that summer.

It began a few weeks after I had failed Grade Three, when a tall man with a white cane knocked on the back door. I was upstairs, and guessing he was there to talk about me, I stayed quiet like before and listened. And, yes, he was there to talk about me.

It was more like a tug of war than a talk. Mr. Wood from the Institute for the Blind, the CNIB, was on one side of the rope, pleading for Mom to enrol me at the School for the Blind in Halifax. Mom was on the other end, pulling with all her might that I stay put. Upstairs, I was on Mom's side, quietly cheering her on. I would have pulled on the rope myself, I was so afraid of going back to school, whether up the street or in some faraway place called Halifax.

"Gone for months at a time and *that* far from home!" Mom repeated while sobbing, "I can't do that, I'm sorry, maybe when he's older." Eventually, Mom won the battle and I breathed a sigh of relief.

A few weeks later there was another tug of war with the same result and yet another in early August and that was to be it. But the "it" was not what I or even Mom had expected. After another tug of war with the same result and just when Mr. Wood was preparing to leave, he turned around and said something I thought was cruel at the time because it made my mother cry.

"Mrs. Mercer," he said in a firm voice, "I don't mean to be harsh but when Robert grows up, he'll know it was *his* parents who denied him an education." In the time it took for me to think I'd never do that, it was too late.

"Give me the papers, please," Mom replied, crying even louder this time. "I'll sign them right now!" What changed her mind, I don't know, but Mom always regretted not being educated herself, much past Grade Three, and that probably had something to do with it. I'm sure, too, that Dad wanted me in school and Mom would have known that as well.

The fact that Mr. Wood was blind and remarkably independent had more to do with the final outcome than all the words spoken. It showed my mother what I might become someday, if educated. That final tug on the rope by Mr. Wood was difficult for Mom to hear and, no doubt, just as hard for him to say, but it worked.

For me, it marked the end of a difficult summer. Of what was to follow, I had no idea. It was back to school and away from home for months at a time: that I knew. And as much as it bothered me, I never once told Mom or Dad that I didn't want to go.

As it were, I was darned lucky that Mr. Wood from the CNIB was not the sort to give up before a final tug on the rope, a few well-chosen words in the right place. Now, whenever I need advice on anything to do with blindness, I look for people like Mr. Wood, people who travel the world on the same or nearly the same path.

For the next two weeks, as much as Mom would have liked me to stay home, she made the "blind school," as she called it, sound more like a summer camp than a school. She boasted of parties all the time, new friends, and fresh milk every day. It sounded good all right, but still I just wanted to stay home. Mom played it up so often and with such enthusiasm that, come a thousand more schools, I wasn't about to let her down. Besides, I was old enough at nine to know that I'd have to go.

CHAPTER FIVE

I turned ten in late August. Before I left for the School in Halifax, there was a farewell birthday party like no other. All the kids from all around were there, a few I knew and most I didn't. The cake, I liked; the games, not so much, but the gift from my grandmother: that I'd never forget. It was a brand-new transistor radio and it was to be my companion for years to come. And it wasn't just any radio: it was battery-charged with transistors instead of tubes. You could carry it and listen to it anywhere.

On the Labour Day weekend, party over, we departed for Halifax, Earl and I, Mom and Dad. We left in a car with a friend of the family because Dad, all his life, was too nervous to drive. He never looked nervous to me, but, apparently, he was nervous about driving and a lot of other things as well. That ended up inside of me, too. In those days I was afraid of my own shadow, of cars and trains, crossing the street and pretty well anything that made a loud noise. Surprisingly, though, I didn't mind the drive to Halifax.

The next day we arrived at the old School on University Avenue. It was the first school for the blind in Canada, opening its doors in 1871 to four students only and thousands more since then. I didn't know and wouldn't have believed it either, but that School, as old as it was, was to be my home and classroom for the next nine years, with time home at Christmas, Easter, and summer holidays.

A jolly man with a big stomach and keys rattling in his pockets, Mr. Hawes, the Head Supervisor on the boys' side, greeted us at the main door and off we went on a tour of the biggest house I had ever seen. Mr. Hawes spoke in a coarse, gravelly voice, hardly finishing a sentence without needing a breath of air. He was old from where I stood that morning, probably already in his sixties.

The building and the school grounds took up the whole city block. Ceilings were higher than two or three rooms up and most of the walls were either panelled in dark wood or cream and green paint.

The main entrance was bright and carpet-soft underfoot and almost cheerful. It was mostly offices at the entrance and directly upstairs was the nursing station and hospital ward. Instead of going up and through the faint smell of medicines that filled the stairwell, we walked past the offices and into a T-shaped corridor.

To the left was the girls' residence where a big grandfather clock stood tall, as if on guard. To the right was the boys' wing, a home away from home for as many as ninety boys at a time. Before going there, we walked straight ahead and down a long corridor. Off to the right was a Braille library and a few small classrooms, and, straight ahead, the main school building.

The corridor that got us there was brightly lit with windows, all the way down, and weird rubbery plants in huge green pots on both sides. It was like a jungle without snakes and monkeys—or none that I could see. I never got to like those plants. But like them or not, they're fixed in the memory of most kids who lived at the school, some who liked them and at least one who didn't.

We continued straight ahead to the main school building. It was paneled in dark hardwood with worn-down wooden floors that creaked with every step. To the left was the Principal's office and, straight ahead, classrooms on both sides. Beyond that was the Juniors' residence where the younger kids lived, some as young as five; and none without lots of memories about home.

There was a small gymnasium in the basement, a large playroom, a woodworking shop for the boys, and a room for the girls to do what girls do in Domestic Science. I had no idea what Domestic Science was, nor what the girls did there, and I didn't think to ask.

The smell of wood stain, forever fixed in my memory of the old School, greeted us as we walked upstairs to a full-sized auditorium with a stage and a floor-to-ceiling pipe organ. The auditorium was filled with wooden seats joined together in long rows with an aisle down the middle. If not for the absence of church benches and an altar, you'd think it was a church.

Surrounding the churchlike auditorium were small piano rooms for practicing and larger rooms belonging to the music teachers. There was another level above that, with more little rooms and more pianos, some broken-down for teaching piano tuning. I didn't know what that was either, and, like before, I didn't think to ask.

The classroom building, top to bottom, was Dickensian, but, back then, having just turned ten, I hadn't heard of Charles Dickens, so it was just old, dark, and creaky.

We spent the rest of the morning in the boys' residence. Mr. Hawes spoke to Earl and me as much as to Mom and Dad and that made me feel a bit better. Nevertheless, with everyone still there, I was already feeling alone. *They wouldn't really leave me here,* I thought to myself.

The boys' residence had four levels; the main floor, two floors of dormitories above, and a basement below. On the main floor, ground level, was a large TV and games room, the Supervisor's office, a room for smoking, and a large office belonging to Mrs. Allen, the wife of the man in charge, the school Superintendent. Every now and then, a boy would pass by, a few using the wall as guide and some running. All told, the ground floor was brightly lit, as welcoming a place as possible for a century-old building.

From the ground floor a staircase with huge spindles wound its way upstairs to four large dormitories, a bus-station-sized washroom, a sewing room, and a few private bedrooms for the older boys and the few staff who lived at the School.

The rooms were nothing like at home. Ceilings were higher than one room on top of another, the wooden floors creaked, and, wherever space allowed, there were pipes and radiators, hot ones and cold ones, all newly painted in the creams and greens of old hospitals.

As the upstairs was just about the same, we didn't bother. My dorm was the second one on the floor, facing the stairs, and it was filled with iron-frame beds, all neatly made and one alongside the other. In front of the beds was a wall of plywood lockers with no locks. A large window at the very end looked out over the playground and brought in the light. The room was bright and clean, and, if not for so many beds so close together, and wooden floors, it might have been more inviting.

Farther along the hall and off to the right was a long, narrow washroom with almost as many sinks as pianos in the other building. From what I could see, there were no private bathroom stalls, no showers or places to take a bath without being seen.

By then, I just wanted to leave. I couldn't imagine waking up in that place without Mom to help me get ready for school. Today, I'd describe the residence as a nineteenth-century English boarding school waiting for a makeover.

I saw one boy who was totally blind walking along the wall to the staircase where, to my great surprise, he leaned on the railing and slid all the way down to the main floor, without touching the steps. I would certainly come to enjoy doing that over the years.

When it was time for Mom, Dad, and Earl to leave for home, as fearful as I was, I let on it was okay and made doubly sure not to cry. Mom did the same, but not so well. Saying good-bye to Earl was no easier. He was quiet, too, like me, and probably wanted to get me out of there as well, but, like me, he wouldn't have said so. Earl, more than anyone, made up for what I didn't see when younger.

Dad was his usual quiet self and did his best, in a few words, to lessen the worry. "You'll like it here, Robert," he said with a hand on my shoulder, "and don't worry, you'll be home soon." Mr. Hawes repeated the "soon" part, but I was far too young to imagine four months passing that quickly or even at all. Then it was hugs, kisses, and handshakes all around. A few blinks later, like music fading out, they were gone.

I filled up and thought about running after them, but I couldn't face giving up that soon. If I had, they would not have left me there, I'm sure. Instead, I took a deep breath and went upstairs to unpack. Every item in the suitcase came with some memory of home, and, worst of all, it brought to mind the day when Mom and I went shopping for new clothes at Spinners in downtown Sydney. It was clothes on credit, paid down just in time to buy more the following year. And poor Earl, he always got the hand-me-downs.

All I could think about at the time was not being in the back seat of the car with Earl on the drive home. I can't describe how it felt to be that alone and so empty. It was a kind of sickness that couldn't go away, no matter what was said or done. You knew inside that you'd be home again, but still, four months away was almost forever.

I lay down and sobbed until the buzzer sounded for supper. Two other boys were in the dorm, five beds down, playing cards and laughing.

"You wanna play," one of the boys asked, but even with that, I didn't have the strength to get up. In nine years at the School, I never unpacked without feeling that same sickly emptiness, although, later on, it was milder and shorter-lived.

When a buzzer rang, I followed the boys down two flights of stairs to the basement, through a long corridor and into a large dining room, which by then was almost filled. The boys were standing at tables as if sorted by age. I went to the same table as the two boys from my dorm. An older boy was asked to say grace. I remember lots of talking and laughing around the table but not much more. I doubt if I was good company but I must have done okay because after dinner I spent the rest of the evening with the two boys, playing cards until bedtime.

When alone or at bedtime I cried, and did so for a few weeks, thinking that if I cried hard and long enough, they'd let me go home. For a time, I honestly thought I was going to win that battle, but no matter what I did, I was there to stay, at least until Christmas.

Supervisors and other staff stopped by from time to time, and I don't know why, but that made me even more determined to keep on crying until they sent me home. An older boy from my hometown of Sydney, by the name of John Eves, heard me crying and used to say, "I cried too, Robert, but look at me, I'm not crying now. It'll soon go away, I promise." And like an older brother, he checked on me from time to time until the crying stopped.

That first day at the School was not one I like to remember. The feeling of being lost, missing my family, and the apprehension of what would happen next was almost unbearable. But somehow, as if all the woes of past schools had come together to make amends, something long overdue was about to happen to me on the very next day, Monday, the first day of school.

CHAPTER SIX

On Monday at 7:15 a.m., and forever thereafter, we all woke up to the piercing sound of a brass bell, ding-a-linging along from one dorm to another and then up the stairs. Nothing happened at the School without bells, buzzers, and line-ups. We lined up for meals, school in the other building, and church outside. Sometimes, it seemed, we lined up just for the practice of doing it again.

I got up and said good morning to my next-door neighbour and he and I went into the washroom together. As there were maids in the sewing room, opposite the washroom, no one went half-dressed to wash up. I lined up at the row of sinks with other boys from all four dorms on the floor, kids nine to twelve or thereabouts. There was some talking in front of the mirrors but mostly someone humming a tune or singing a song. I was less afraid than I thought I would be, and even without Mom, I had everything ready so as not to be late for school. I washed up and combed my hair and went back to the dorm to put things away.

After cleaning up and lining up for a blob of cod liver oil, it was downstairs to line up for breakfast. We marched down another flight of stairs and into the basement, two by two, through an underground tunnel, past the Juniors' dining room and into ours. With pipes of all sizes either hugging the walls of the tunnel or clinging to the ceiling, it could have been, as I imagined from time to time, an entrance to an underground bomb shelter, or, better still, a secret passageway to the very centre of the earth.

The dining room was mostly painted in white and light blue. Fluorescent lights attached themselves to a low ceiling that you could reach up and touch. There were tables for four, and, farther in, a smaller room with two longer tables, all nicely set and ready.

The eggs might have been a bit rubbery, the toast soggy, and the top slice of bread a bit stale, but overall, the food at the School was better than good on most days and always plentiful. Today I'd gladly sit down to Mrs. Woodward's fish and chips every second Friday, Sunday dinners with homemade pie, her beef gravy from real beef, or the pancakes we got once a year. As good as it was, and as often as we were told about starving children in Africa (always Africa), lots of food was left over.

It you didn't like porridge or cream of wheat for breakfast, you could fill up on cold cereal with fresh milk, not the powdered kind. If salt cod and potatoes for dinner on Mondays was not to your liking, you could get by with bread and real butter. And if that wasn't enough, it was only a few hours to the next meal.

I can almost recite the weekly menu by heart, as it hardly ever changed in my nine years at the School. It was so reliable, week to week, that if you didn't want the pears served at Tuesday supper, you could trade them, in advance, to someone who didn't like homemade pie at Sunday dinner. And with more than ninety boys enrolled at the School, you could always find someone who didn't like your favourite dessert.

On that first morning, I sat with Tony MacNeil and two other boys from my dorm. It was Tony's first year at the School as well, but it didn't seem to bother him nearly as much. We talked and laughed during break-fast about nothing I can remember. The dining room was always abuzz with chatter, at and between the tables. I learned quickly that if you wanted something you had to raise your hand and, before long, one of the maids was there.

Tony was a rougher sort than me, not a bully, but closer to that than far away, but I liked him for not being shy or mousy about anything. If you needed someone to do something daring, it was Tony, not me. I glued myself to him for a few days until I knew my way around. As if it was meant to be, we were both in the same class, Grade Three.

After breakfast on that Monday morning I went back upstairs to brush my teeth and get ready for school. After washing the sheets (I'll get to that later), I went downstairs to line up for school, while one of the supervisors checked a list to make sure everyone was there.

I remember feeling less upset already because no one had teased me on the way there or anywhere else the day before. We marched from the boys' side to the main corridor and stopped in front of the girls' lineup. When a buzzer sounded, both lineups turned into the main hall and off we went, through the little jungle and into the School building.

It was girls on one side, boys on the other, and lots of chattering along the way. I saw kids of all ages and many of them with disabilities far worse than mine. Some walked with great difficulty, muscle and body spasms they couldn't control and others in braces. One of the boys near me was almost non-communicative: there but not there. Most of the kids, however, were just totally blind or just partially sighted like me. I didn't notice at the time but there were no kids in wheelchairs, and none in later years either. I was too young not to stare; I had never seen what I saw that morning. And I was surprised to discover that I wasn't as badly off as I thought.

Not long after, we were all seated in the auditorium for what someone told me and Tony was Assembly Hall, held every school day. And there, too, it was girls on one side and boys on the other. I remember how friendly the other kids were, explaining what to expect and what to do next.

I was already talking to some of the other students and picking this one or that one as a possible friend. I don't know why exactly, but I tended to identify with kids like Tony, who seemed to see as well or nearly as well as I did. I certainly wouldn't have thought less of anyone, not me, but that's the way it was.

Then all the students were there in the auditorium, along with some of the teachers and a few of the staff. There was a lot of talking, laughing, and then someone on stage playing a piece on the grand piano, music I recognized from the radio.

I remember how nice it all felt, warm inside, just sitting there in the rows with the other kids, living in the same world, so to speak. As poor as my eyesight was, there were countless others with far less to guide them. For the first time ever, by contrast, I was more sighted than blind.

When a man in a grey suit walked onto the stage, the place turned quiet and we stood up for God Save the Queen, the Lord's Prayer, and a hymn. I knew some of the hymn from church and every word of the Lord's Prayer from school, except for what the Protestants added at the end. You'd never hear those words at the end of the Lord's Prayer where I came from. Protestants and Catholics had their own schools and churches and seldom even walked on the same side of the street to get there. I'm not sure I ever met a real Protestant before then and, of course, they were just like us, not as whispered about at home.

The man on stage introduced himself as Mr. Allen, the School Superintendent. He welcomed us to another year of study and, after a few announcements, he opened a book and began Chapter One of *The Wind in the Willows*. He read to us every day. If it wasn't that book, it was *Alice in Wonderland* or *Tom Sawyer* or *Gulliver's Travels*.

On that first morning and years of mornings thereafter, Mr. Allen read to us like he himself had written the books. It was one chapter a day until the end of that book and the beginning of the next. The readings were just like movies come to life and yet chock full of lessons and characters to be remembered.

Mr. Allen spoke like the Badger or Toad or the Ghost of Christmas Past. And as entertaining as it was back

then, it's even more so now. A good teacher is appreciated when they teach you, but even more as time moves
forward. I never had much to do with Mr. Allen (or the
Ghost of Christmas Past, either), but, whenever I did,
he was kind and yet firm, formal and yet friendly, like
you'd expect of someone in charge.

Sitting to my left was Donald Keeping, an older kid
who was totally blind. I stared at him as he read the
hymn with his fingers. I'd heard of Braille before, but
to see it working: that was amazing. When he put the
words down, I picked them up and ran my finger over
the pages. I felt the bumps, which, of course, made no
sense to me, whether up, down, or sideways.

After leaving the School years later I realized that
nothing was done there without some thoughtful
purpose. Morning Assembly gave us a sense of belonging to a larger community and the readings made
up for books we probably would have read, but with
great difficulty. Even the bells and buzzers taught
me always to be on time. I was feeling better already
and that was just the beginning of my first day at the
School for the Blind in Halifax.

CHAPTER SEVEN

Tony and I walked together to the Grade Three class-room. When there, I looked around and saw no rows upon rows of school desks, just long tables with chairs behind. We made our way to the table furthest from the blackboard, and before we could even sit down, a girl with glasses and blond hair came over and said hello. Her name was Nina Higgins and I can't remember what I said back or what Tony said either, but I had a new friend and she was a lot prettier than Tony.

It wasn't like me to go around the room and say hello to the other kids as they arrived, two or three at a time. Some of them, as I learned later on, had known each other since Kindergarten. I remember Martin Collicutt as one of the more affable kids, never shy to say hello or laugh at anything even remotely funny. I can still see Valerie Beaulieu and Rita Arsenault, arriving together, as they did for years afterward, still good friends to this day.

As I recall, everyone in the class had some degree of useful vision, more or less than me. When the teacher arrived and started class, there were nine of us in total. *That's odd,* I thought, *only nine pupils.* In my first try at Grade Three in public school, there were forty of us, at least.

The teacher's name was Mrs. Beaton, and I can still see her on that first morning, dressed in a light green blouse and a dark green skirt. It's like a photo, fixed in my memory, with the same smile, too, like it was meant for me. I could tell she was a nice person, just from the sun-shiny way she shouted, "Welcome to Grade Three!" like we had all won something.

After roll call, Mrs. Beaton came over and spoke directly to me. "Robert," she began, "stand up, please, and tell the class where you come from." I was startled. No teacher had ever spoken to me first—or tenth for that matter. I would have struggled to stutter out something if she hadn't continued, "And, Robert, I'll need your address as well for my records."

She said "Robert" like she knew me, so I stood up, raised my voice, and answered her like it was my last chance ever. "I'm from Sydney, Cape Breton, and my address is 778 Grand Lake Road."

At that very moment, I felt instantly better, as if a

warm light was shining on me, and me alone: I was that excited and pleased with myself. An overwhelming feeling of relief washed over me.

It doesn't sound like much, I know—"name and address"—but, for me, it was far more than just the right answer to a simple answer. It was me, standing up and speaking aloud, like I belonged there. I had no recollection, before then, of ever being asked a question in front of a class.

Thankfully, and because of the question, I felt like a kid with a hundred chances to swing at the ball. I was feeling that lost and alone before the question, and that much better afterward. Of course, I didn't know what an epiphany moment was back in Grade Three, but I had one then, and it was to change my life.

And if that wasn't enough to get me started, Mrs. Beaton hardly ever used the blackboard, and, when she did, it was more for her to follow than for us to read. She did things close-up, so we could see what she was doing, like a good writer does: showing the reader and not just telling the story. That mattered a lot to me, not having to strain to see what she was doing, and not a worry as to what I might have missed.

After everyone else had introduced themselves— some voices too quiet for me to hear—it wasn't long before Mrs. Beaton spoke to each of us by name, as if she had known us since birth. And when she talked directly to me or anyone else, she'd lean over and speak, face to face, and that made me feel like she meant it, whatever it was.

The warm light that shone on me in the First Period grew even brighter in the Second Period, doing sums, when Mrs. Beaton leaned over and whispered, "You're doing fine, Robert, keep it up." It was like my mother would have done, and if she could have been there, just for that first morning, she would have slept a whole lot better from then on.

If I needed help, I raised my hand and there was Mrs. Beaton. I didn't ask a lot of questions for a while, but once I did, I wasn't about to slow down. I got more gold and silver stars that first week than all the years before, and every time I got one, I felt that much better inside. I even got to like the red and blue ones.

In these simple ways, Mrs. Beaton turned me around to face the world, head on, maybe sensing my unease, or perhaps just being a good teacher. I'm sure Mrs. Flynn, my Grade Three teacher in public school, would have done just as much, had she had only nine students instead of forty.

The fact that the other kids in the classroom were also visually impaired was no small factor in the final equation. It put me at ease, on an equal footing. I wouldn't have described myself as competitive in the least, but now, on a level playing field, that, too, was possible. I soon discovered how competitive I was by nature, always wanting to get one of those gold stars. I wanted to do well, and having a good chance at it, I wanted to do even better. I'd given up on that in my previous school, a long time ago, and now it was back. It was a nice feeling.

By recess that morning, I had gone from disliking school to embracing it, knowing then that I could learn like everyone else. After that, I morphed into a real student, excited about doing my sums or pleased to show my latest drawing. We did a lot of drawings in Grade Three and googols of sums.

The first three periods, about forty minutes each, passed quickly before the buzzer sounded for recess at 11:15. I enjoyed that, too, back in the TV room with Tony and Gary Grant, another new student from two grades above me.

Most times during recess we either watched television or went upstairs to the dorm, where there was always someone playing a guitar, playing cards, or just huddling around a radio; there were no TV's in the dorm. Although a lot more time would pass before I was fully settled in, I was no longer feeling like the odd kid at the front of the class.

When back in the classroom for the Fourth Period, someone knocked on the door and told Mrs. Beaton it was our turn to go to the Principal's office for school supplies. Mrs. Beaton told us what to get and off we went.

The lady in the Principal's office was sent there, I'm sure, to teach all of us a lesson in "waste not, want not." She gave each of us one less of almost everything we were told to get. "Four scribblers," she told me, "is enough for now and you can have another when they're all filled."

The Fourth Period might have been reading class or spelling or writing, I don't remember. If it was reading class, we had books with large print. For spelling, I remember mostly drills, spelling out loud. In mathematics, we did written sums, and we did a lot of mental math over the years, the thinking being that with poor eyesight, you couldn't just pick up a pencil and get the answer.

When the old grandfather clock at the main entrance sounded the noonday chimes, the morning was still not over. Class was not adjourned for lunch until a fifth period was over at 12:55 p.m.

When the buzzer rang for lunch, Mrs. Beaton asked me to clean the blackboard. And even something as unremarkable as that made me feel better. I cleaned a lot of blackboards after that, developing my own technique, always left to right, one manageable chunk at a time, so as not to miss a spot. But the real treat, as I recall it, was to clean a blackboard with a wet cloth, uncovering how unbelievably clean it still was, underneath.

And that was how, for the most part, my first few classes at the School for the Blind unfolded. I didn't know what to expect in the beginning, beyond showing up to find out. But when I did, nothing could have been more uplifting. I got a full dose of self-esteem and confidence—enough for a lifetime.

As I see it now, that first morning with Mrs. Beaton was my first "real" time at school. Of course, I knew a lot of things from before, because I could hear, but now, at the School for the Blind, I could see as well.

I didn't think of it in Grade Three, or for years later, but the matter of being educated, in my case, was left entirely to chance: the chance that a teacher in public school would take a stand; the chance that a blind person from the CNIB would not give up after more than one visit; that my parents would let me go; or even that people, one hundred years earlier, had seen the good sense of educating children who were blind. And even with that, without the right teacher at the right time, Mrs. Beaton, I would have found some way to get back home and never return.

Mrs. Beaton taught at the School for only one year and it just happened to be my first. I would like to have followed her career but kids don't usually think that way.

CHAPTER EIGHT

Lunch was called "dinner" at the School, not that it matters, but it struck me as a bit out of place. I couldn't get used to it back then, so let it be "lunch" from now on. Lunch was also the biggest meal of the day, and after that first morning at school with Mrs. Beaton, and not having eaten much the day before, I gobbled the salt cod with potatoes and carrots like it was Chinese food.

The dining room was like another world within the School. For one thing, all the boys were there at the same time, from me in Grade Three to those studying for graduation in Grade Eleven. It was a noisy room and yet, seated at tables for four, it wasn't that hard to hear. Seeing large pitchers of fresh milk at every table, and dishes of real butter, I was wishing my brother was there.

I can't recall exactly where I went after lunch, but

on a typical day, before noticing the girls, I would have been outside with the other kids, playing hockey with a tin can, wrestling or playing baseball, the same fun and games I did at home with Earl.

The school playground was more like a park with a wrought-iron fence all around. The far end of the property, facing South Street, was like a section of the Public Gardens, with tall mature trees, lilac bushes, and a walking path of grey crushed stone, around the perimeter. I hardly went there in Grade Three, but, later on, when walking hand in hand with a girlfriend was the highlight of the day, I walked marathons.

We had a sand lot for playing baseball in the fall and spring, easily converted to an ice rink in the winter. There was some playground equipment for the younger kids, but I only remember the dark green jungle gym that managed, every winter, to freeze someone's tongue to its iron bars. It happened every year, I'm sure, but only once per kid.

Around the school building, inside the fence, there was a sidewalk and a small area paved in asphalt, directly in front of the Juniors' residence.

When I was twelve, I was on that asphalt late one night, smoking a cigarette with a friend of mine, when, suddenly, a bright light was flashing in my eyes. "Put out those cigarettes and come with me." It was one of our supervisors.

When inside the building, he brought us up to the office and explained that it was Mr. Allen, the Superintendent, who saw the flickers of light in the dark, through his binoculars. And without explaining any further, he told us first to stop smoking, and, secondly, that if we had to smoke, to do so on the other side of the building, away from Mr. Allen's house. What a surprise that was, an unusual form of discipline, but well received, nonetheless.

On rainy days, we congregated in the TV room, in the dorm, or in the classrooms. The lunch break ended when the buzzer sounded for a sixth period at 2:30 p.m. The sixth and seventh periods were taken up with more of the three Rs, but that wasn't the end of the day, as it would have been in public school.

There were three more periods, the eighth and ninth, which I spent down in the woodworking shop. The tenth period was marked "free," which you seldom got in the higher grades.

In the woodworking shop, we were taught one on one, and, in that first week, I learned to cut a lion free from a block of wood. I had sanded it down to the size of a kitten by the time it had passed Mr. Burgher's inspection. In the months that followed, I learned to make wooden toys, to cane and rope chairs, to make mats from coarse twine, and to use power tools without losing fingers.

The boys' workshop was in a large room with work benches lined up, side by side, right back to the far wall on the left. To the right was a heavy-duty lathe, and scattered throughout the room were power tools of all kinds, from jigsaws to drills to the loud and scary bench saws. It was a statement of normalcy within the School, a way of showing us that most anything is possible with due care and proper training. In time, I got to know all those saws and what they could do, and, despite the risk of accidents, there were none, as I recall, beyond a splinter or two.

The work benches were filled with interesting projects in various stages of work, and helter-shelter about the room were chairs in all stages of being roped or caned, and twine mats still on the frame. I saw the workshop as a place to play, I liked it that much. I felt at home in that playroom and why not: my grandfather was a carpenter; Dad could build a house literally from the ground up; and likewise for my brothers, Earl and Brian.

Nina and the other girls from Grade Three would have been just as busy in Domestic Science, learning to cook, sew, knit, crochet, or whatever other manual skills might be useful later on, either for working at home or in the workplace.

On that first evening of school, I spent most of my free time in the TV room. There was one channel only, CBC, the same as at home and with all the same programs. A few more years would pass before even CTV was on the scene, offering, as I remember most, a Wednesday night hockey game to rival Saturday's Hockey Night in Canada on the CBC. You had to be there with one channel and nothing but a test pattern until 4:30 p.m. to fully appreciate the excitement of another network.

I played checkers that evening with Clifford Clayton and never once beat him in the few years we played, but no one else did either. Clifford was one of a few black kids to enrol at the School, one year younger than me but more like an older brother, being so strong and athletic. If you ended up on his side, no matter what the sport, you'd come out on top. And, by the way, kids were teased like at any school, but never because of skin colour, as I remember it.

A few weeks later, I even watched the New York Yankees win the World Series, with Hall of Fame players like Mickey Mantle, Whitey Ford, and Yogi Berra. An older boy, Brian Lucas, was in the TV room for every game, and he told me all about his team, the Baltimore Orioles. I'm still an Oriole fan and for no other reason than that.

On that first day of school, I filled up more than once when thinking about home, and I cried myself to sleep for days after, but I had turned a corner that morning in Mrs. Beaton's class. My whole world had been turned upside down in just a few days. There I was, unlike my former self, liking school, dreading long weekends with little to do, enjoying homework, and talking to lots of kids. I was still very shy and withdrawn, but as the days passed, there were fewer tears and less time for thinking about home.

Bedtime for Grade Three was 8:30 p.m. and it took me a while to get used to that. Most nights before lights out, Mr. Hawes would lead us in the same prayer as always: "Now I lay me down to sleep..." He never left the dorm without hollering back: "You boys keep your hands above the sheets and go to sleep." As soon as the jingle of the keys in his pocket faded away, we didn't dare get up, but talking and laughing was far from over and sleep not far from that.

When Mr. Hawes was in a good mood, it was like summer camp in the dorm. We'd gather around or just lay in bed while he read to us. He seemed always to pick the kind of books that kept us waiting for the next chapter. We'd live in Africa one week with Bomba the Jungle Boy, and the next week, back in Nova Scotia, with one of Helen Creighton's Bluenose Ghosts. And once in a while, he'd pass around cookies and loose candies, or, on the best days, chocolate bars.

As he read, it was like the ghosts were in the room, waiting for the end of the chapter and lights out.

CHAPTER NINE

As the Juniors' dining room was on the way to ours, we saw the little kids, some as young as five, every day. They marched by us, two by two, with dedicated staff like Ruth Connors leading the way. They never passed us by without getting lots of attention. It didn't make up for them being lonely or us missing a younger sibling at home, but it was enough for lots of laughs and smiles, back and forth.

The first morning at school with Mr. Allen and Mrs. Beaton had put me on the right path, but there was another big problem in my way. I was still wetting the bed at age ten and had to wash the sheets in front of everyone in the bathroom before going to school. It was almost as bad as the teasing at my other schools but I wasn't the only one and I was not the oldest by far.

It was two weeks of that awful routine until one

morning I was called out of class and told to report to the nurse's station. I had no idea for what and neither did the messenger. When I got there, a motherly nurse talked to me like the day was meant for me. After helping me onto a bed table, she introduced the doctor and he, too, was friendly and talkative.

When he finished, mostly pressing down on the muscles in my lower back, he looked me straight in the face and said, "Robert, I promise you that from now on you'll not be wetting the bed, ever again." I thought at first that he was telling *me* to promise *him,* but, no, *he* promised *me,* and from then on it was good morning sunshine and good riddance to nocturnal enuresis: bedwetting. I don't know what he did exactly or why it worked, but it did, and, after that, I got to make my bed each morning with the other kids.

I'm sure the School thought that a well-dressed bed made for a happy day—or at least for a neat and tidy room in case of visitors. All the beds were exactly the same: single, iron-framed with white fold-down sheets and a rust-brown, woollen cover. It was twelve or so beds to a dorm, no more than two feet apart, and a bunk bed or two when too many sardines enrolled for the same can. It was hospital corners all around and new sheets once a week. Clothes were marked in indelible ink, mostly by mothers at home, picked up on Thursdays and delivered the next day.

One of the boys in the dorm next to mine walked in his sleep and I can't remember whether it was that year or the one following, but one night he sleep-walked right out the window and fell two storeys to the ground. Apart from a broken arm, he was fine and, like me, never to wet the bed again, he never again walked in his sleep.

On the weekends, my new friend, Gary, signed me out and we travelled the streets of Halifax, walking miles to every car dealership we could find. Gary loved cars more than food and for a time even more than girls. In our travels, we collected colourful brochures on every car in the showroom and every model, too. Gary knew all of them by heart and whenever he said "Wow!" I looked around, expecting to see a girl walk by, but it was just another car.

I took it all in and remembered none of it, having no interest in cars whatsoever. But that wasn't the point; Halifax was a big city, I loved to walk, and I had a friend to lead the way. Gary was old enough at thirteen to leave the School premises and old enough to sign me out as well. Letting on that I was interested in cars was a small price to pay for all the walking we did and the fun we had over the next few weeks and for years after that.

When thirteen or in Grade Seven, the boys could go out and off the School property by themselves. The girls were less fortunate, not allowed off the school grounds until all of sixteen and, even then, only with two other girls of the same age or older.

In that first month or two at the School, I grew up plenty. Gradually, the homesickness went into hibernation and I surfaced, no longer feeling inferior or left out. I was still very shy and withdrawn and, although I hid that away when older, it's still very much a part of who I am. Regardless, I'd made it, but not without a lot of help!

Apart from the good things happening in the classroom and new friends, there was that transistor radio my grandmother had given me on my tenth birthday, just before I left for Halifax. It cost her more than she could easily afford but she knew all about being homesick, having left her family in Lebanon when only fifteen, never to get back. She knew I'd need something to get by.

Before long I knew every song on the hit parade. I listened to baseball games from Baltimore, hockey games, and even the news, once in a while. It brought other kids to me, kids who heard a song they liked or the siren that told of a goal at Maple Leaf Gardens or the Montreal Forum. In later years it was evening programs and plays on the CBC.

I learned a lot from that radio and, more than that, it helped me to stop thinking about home, "out of

ROBERT MERCER

mind, out of me." If I could go back there today, grown up, I'd make sure every kid had a radio and I'd make sure this time that my grandmother knew how much it meant to me.

It took a lot of time but, eventually, I got good at not thinking about home. I felt guilty but it was so much better than being homesick. Sometimes days and later on weeks would pass with not more than a few thoughts of home.

It was a great help for me as well to see older boys showing the way forward by just being there and doing what older boys do. No matter how visually impaired they were, and many of them totally blind, they did things I thought incredible, like playing the piano, building model ships in woodworking class, writing and reading Braille, running a student newspaper or a drama club, and having girlfriends as well. When I looked up at them, I knew why I was there. I didn't wish it but I knew why.

In a way, most everyone there, at one time or another, was a student, a teacher, an older sister or brother, a guardian, or just a friend to someone else, as my friend John Eves who adopted me for a few weeks when I first arrived. He didn't have to watch over me and may not even remember it, but, in so doing, he taught me to do the same.

Many of us read letters from home to kids who

54

couldn't read and I can't count the times that one of the older boys helped me with my homework, or how often I did the same for kids, older and younger alike. On the ice rink and on the dance floor, I tried to give some attention to the girls who seldom got asked.

One of the older boys showed me how to use the Gestetner to copy pages for the School newspaper. I was warned about the ink but no matter how careful you were, you were sure to ruin a shirt or waste an hour afterward trying to wash it off.

One evening during study period, Noel Brown, one of the older students, saw me and a friend of mine looking at an ad for maps in a magazine. "It's a nice way to learn geography," Noel said. "Go ahead and order them and I'll pay the $9.99." The maps arrived a few weeks later and, for the rest of that year, Grade Five, and maybe the next, maps of seven continents covered the classroom walls, each adorned with copper-coloured stickers where copper was mined, silver ones for silver, and so on. I never think of those maps without thinking how kind it was for Noel to have done that; it was a lot of money in those days, even for an older boy.

Examples like these speak to one of the most important aspects of the School: not just the blind helping the blind, but one member of a large family looking out for another. Even in that first year at the School, I could turn to Brian Lucas, John Eves, or a host of other kids if I needed help, and sometimes just a kind word or a simple "hello" passed from one person to another made the difference.

As the weeks passed, I found it less difficult and more fun to be there. I was no longer the only one in the crowd who couldn't see the blackboard and being with kids like myself, that brought out the best in me. Life was far less stressful and there was always a chance of finishing the race and possibly even coming first for a change. And, yes, there were parties, too, but not every day as Mom had promised.

CHAPTER TEN

That first day of class with Mrs. Beaton was a call for me to wake up and get on with being a kid. It shucked me out of my shell and into the daily routine of living and learning at my new school in Halifax. I spoke with other kids and the staff and, lots of times, I spoke first.

Two doors down from my homeroom was a class of junior kids, Grade One, I think. Having younger brothers and sisters of my own I never walked by without peeking in on the little ones. One morning, when Mrs. Beaton was home sick, I had a free period and was ambling along the hallway and doing the usual peeking-in when, suddenly, the door opened. It was Mrs. Casey, the Grade One teacher.

"Come in, come in," she insisted, "I could use some help this morning if you're not busy." *Help,* I thought, *me, help a teacher?* She introduced me as "Robert, a boy from Grade Three," like the class should be impressed and, of course, they actually were: all four of them.

For the next half hour or so I helped the teacher pass around handfuls of miniature objects. There were little telephone poles, church steeples, houses, garden tools, and more.

I could tell right away that these kids were either totally blind or at least far more visually impaired than I was. While they talked over what the objects might be, I remember thinking how great it was that they were here, learning, laughing, and having fun, not somewhere else, up close and still not seeing the blackboard.

As each object was passed around, it was carefully examined by all hands and from all sides while Mrs. Casey explained what it was. Some were easily guessed at, but most were unknown to these kids and some to me as well. It struck me that with poor eyesight, you could bump into a telephone pole all day long and never know what was at the top or how they joined up, or the way houses are aligned on a street or how a chimney could possibly sit upright on a slanted roof.

The kids asked a thousand questions: "What's this pipe at the top of the chimney?" and questions of the like. Hearing the questions taught me to be less timid and more inquisitive about things I couldn't see. Back home I was always embarrassed in class to ask about something everyone else could see.

Being there and helping the teacher: that was me, coming out from behind the shadows. The feeling of confidence that came with me that morning was another big piece of the puzzle, the one you don't know is missing until you feel it.

A month or so later there was a terrible coal-mining disaster at Springhill, Nova Scotia. Seventy-five miners perished more than 4,000 feet below the surface. Of the many who were saved, some had been trapped there for as long as nine days without food or water. Thanks to my radio and thanks to my grandmother, I knew everything about the "bump," as they called it.

There was also a song about it on the radio, which I learned with two other boys from my class. We were down in the basement rehearsing the words one day when Mr. Legge, the Principal, overheard us. "Would you boys mind singing that song for one of my teachers?" he asked. I thought for sure I'd mind and I think the other kids did, too, but this was the Principal. A boy nearby was giggling because we had to sing for a teacher.

That teacher was the same Mrs. Casey with the little telephone poles; the same Mrs. Casey who, we came to learn later on, had lost family and close friends in the mining disaster at Springhill.

She cried as we sang but she loved the song and invited us back to sing it two more times that week. I hardly ever spoke to teachers before Mrs. Beaton and Mrs. Casey, but now I was adding and subtracting sums for one and singing to another.

The time outside of school was long at first, mostly on weekends. However, Mr. Hawes did his best to fill in some of the time. He knew everything about fun and games for kids and didn't just watch, he often pitched in, throwing the ball or running the bases. If you couldn't see him, you could hear the keys rattling in his pocket.

He organized baseball games on the School playground, treasure hunts on a nearby hill, and games in the Gym with prizes for everyone. He'd take us to Point Pleasant Park and let us run free among the fortresses or on the beach. He even took us swimming in the freezing cold waters of the North West Arm. And as to "gold in them thar hills," I believed every word of it, no matter how many rusty nails and bottle caps got in the way.

It was during these outings that I saw, firsthand, what kids with vision problems could do, whether baseball, soccer, bowling, skating, swimming, or just fooling around. A few rule changes, here and there, and almost any game becomes possible. From that I learned to think likewise about jobs in the workplace, when I eventually got there.

The School had no religion of its own, apart from

helping us. But most of the kids did, in denominations I didn't know existed. There were Baptists, Presbyterians, Anglicans, and Jehovah's Witnesses. Somewhere in downtown Halifax there was a church to match. For me, it was St. Mary's Basilica on Spring Garden Road.

I marched there for Mass every Sunday with a parade of other Catholics from the School, and likewise for confession every second Saturday. I tried not to sin too much so as not to get the dreaded penance of walking the Stations of the Cross instead of a few Hail Marys. But, in the end, whether a big sin or a little one, you might still get the Stations of the Cross. I never did figure it out.

We were so reliable as young parishioners that the first two rows in the Church were reserved every Sunday just for us Catholics, with boys from the School on one side and girls on the other. And there was that time when one of our kids with Tourette Syndrome stood up in the middle of the sermon and yelled the worst of profanities at the priest. Imagine the penance for that; imagine me, in charge that morning with no idea of what to do. I waited, and, soon enough, he sat quiet and the priest continued.

One of the priests from the same parish came to the School a few nights to teach what most of us already knew about the birds and the bees. One of the boys asked him, seriously, if he knew what a "cherry" was, and without a moment's delay, he replied like he, too, was serious: "I'm sorry, but I don't know anymore, there's not enough cherries in St. Mary's parish to decorate a cake." I certainly enjoyed that one for a time.

The same priest started a Catholic prayer meeting at the School and I was told to attend. At one of these meetings, to my great surprise, we were saying prayers for my mother who was having a baby. I knew that; but I didn't know, until the priest said so, that she was in some difficulty and needed our prayers. And that triggered a new kind of homesickness, one filled with worry. I was told the next day that all had gone well at the hospital, so back I went, from thoughts of home to life at the School.

We got nickels in pancakes on Pancake Day, cookies most nights of the week, and thanks to Chris Stark's parents from the Valley, and other good souls as well, all the students had boxes and boxes of apples and sometimes pears to start off the year.

I got a box of goodies from home on Halloween with candy kisses, hard and soft; caps for my cap gun; and packages of little firecrackers that do their best work in ashtrays filled with beach sand. I got punished for doing that and wasn't allowed outside for a whole week, "off bounds" they called it; but really, it wasn't that bad: no one even thought to ask for the rest of the firecrackers.

I also got letters from Mom and my Grandmother every few weeks and never without a few dollars. I never failed to write back and say "thank you," although hardly ever adding more words than "Hi, hope all is well, everything is fine here." And yet, there was lots of news to tell, all the time.

The School wasn't home, but the staff—most of them—did what they could to make it as much like home as possible. They did a lot more than I noticed or even appreciated at the time. I suppose, as kids, we took a lot for granted, not thinking that Mr. Hawes didn't have to take us out; that Mr. Allen didn't have to read to us at morning Assembly; or that no one had to provide cookies at night or clean tables, neatly set, for every meal in the dining room.

Of course, being young accounts for most of that, but still, I might have been more grateful if I had known then that, back in the late 1800s, the kids at the School tended a cow, grew vegetables, and raised chickens and pigs, in part to learn husbandry—and for the kitchen. In and around the same time, a young girl died of a bad flu at the school, far away from home and family. I'm glad I didn't know that whenever I was sick or lonely. We were fortunate, all right!

CHAPTER ELEVEN

By mid-December it was time, finally, to pack up and go home for Christmas. Back in September, Dad promised I'd be home soon, but there was nothing "soon" about it until the very week before. The sight of suitcases and trunks lining the walls was more exciting for me than the firecrackers at Halloween. But for those who lived too far away to get home at Christmas, it must have been unbearable. I don't know how they survived, children away from home for ten months at a time.

Not surprisingly, the School staff and volunteers organized parties and chartered a bus each year to take the kids out to see the lights and feel the spirit of Christmas. But still, as one of my friends told me, Christmas at the School was just another day, except for Santa and turkey dinner.

My suitcase was there, too, when the bus came to

take us to the train station, there to board the CN train for Sydney. We were a large group, boys and girls together, filling a few train cars: all the kids from Milford Station to Sydney and the ones from Newfoundland as well.

To my great surprise, I actually enjoyed the comfortable seats, the big windows, and the clickety-clack of the train as it travelled from one station to the next. It was the same train I had feared when younger and not the big monster I thought it was, noise and all.

But still, it was a long trip, six hours of moving and three hours of stops along the way. We stopped at every telephone pole, I'm sure, and places too small to mention. But the train ride was also like a party, with bigger happy faces than those painted on a clown. There was a box lunch from the School kitchen and treats for the journey. We played cards and board games, but mostly it was sitting and listening to the radio as one station faded out to make room for another. Away from the city lights, my radio dial came alive with stations from Boston to New York and beyond.

It was never fun when the conductor shouted, "Stewiacke, next stop, Stewiacke." It was the one stop along the way where the train took on more cars and, sometimes, in the cold of winter, we were stopped there for one or two hours.

As the train plodded along I thought of the School and all that had happened in the previous four months. I skipped over the loneliness and thought instead of new friends I'd made, a window I'd broken and didn't mention, the World Series, and even the time I got punished for lighting firecrackers in the ashtrays. The good memories far outweighed the bad and even the bad ones were little, next to those at my other schools.

The closer we got to Sydney, the more excited I got. *Who would be at the station? Who would drive us, and, most of all, would Earl be there? What should I say?* It was excitement beyond words, the other side of homesickness.

Over the years there were lots of kids at the School from Cape Breton, where I came from: fellow train travellers like Valerie Smith from the juniors' side who I watcher over like a younger sister. She was totally blind, bright and smart and one of my favourites. I made sure to say "hello" to her whenever the junior kids passed by on the way to the dining room. There was Rayfield Taylor, a friend who was in my dorm; John Eves who helped me in my first year; and others around my age like Susan and Raymond Young, brother and sister.

When the train whistle sounded and the conductor hollered out, "North Sydney, next stop, North Sydney," I knew I was no more than a half-hour away. To this day, train whistles, no matter where they sound, bring me back to North Sydney and thoughts of going home. Of course, it's not the same home that it was, back in the day, but I feel it just the same.

North Sydney meant farewell to the kids from Newfoundland. From there they'd board the *William Carson* ferry for a long boat ride across the Strait. Even after docking at Port aux Basques, most of the kids were still miles away from home; and days for some, when the winter weather was poor.

For me, it was only one more stop, but getting there was longer than waiting for the bus on Grand Lake Road. By then I had already passed through a number of Sydneys: Sydney Forks, North Sydney, Sydney Mines, and Sydney River—the "Tidneys," as some people call them. When the train finally slowed down to a screeching stop at my Tidney, I was lined up first at the door, suitcase in hand. Mom was on the other side when the door opened. She literally pulled me off the step and hugged me to death, all the while crying out loud that I didn't have to go back to the "blind school," ever again!

She and Dad had talked it over and I could stay home if I wished. Back in September I would have had a quick answer for that, but since then, I'd grown up a lot. I had come through the worst of it and actually gotten to like school, or at least the School for the

Blind in Halifax. At that moment or thereafter, I wasn't about to turn back and give it up.

I couldn't believe my own ears when out sounded, "No Mama, I wanna go back after Christmas. I like it there." And whatever I didn't like, I hid that away and never spoke of it at home.

I wasn't about to mention the homesickness, washing sheets, the few times I was up sick at night, or the many times I was down in the dumps. I said nothing but good things about the School, anything to avoid going back to the one up the street. I don't know where the good sense came from at that moment, but there it was, there when I needed it the most.

Dad was pleased with what I said at the train station; I could tell. He may have said I could stay home, but it was more for Mom, I think. She was often sick with worry about me being away for so long and being that young. I thought I knew then some of what she went through, but, really, I didn't. I didn't understand the depth of it until my own children had reached the age of ten, the age I was when I first left home.

For a time, a day, maybe two, I could have used the F-word at home or tipped over the outhouse and no one would have scolded me. One summer, when just home for the holidays, I told Earl I'd take the blame for something he had done with a baseball and the upstairs window.

Dad was not happy about the broken window but when I told him I had done it by accident, he said, and I quote, "Never mind that, Robert, it's just a pane of glass and some putty." The bloom had worn off the rose when, a few days later, I broke the same window. It was Earl's turn to take the blame; he owed me one.

On the day before Christmas Eve, Earl and I went into the woods in search of the perfect Christmas tree. It was snowing when we left in the morning and by the time we found the right tree, a few hours later and a mile or so into the woods, the snow had piled up and with it came the winds. We dragged that poor tree behind us for a few hours, barely able to see where we were going. By then it was late afternoon, and still no sign of us at home.

When Dad arrived after work he called the RCMP and just when he and some of the neighbours were ready to head out, Eva caught a glimpse of us, dragging the tree through the farmer's field.

If we were lost, we didn't know it and didn't notice either that half the needles on one side of the tree were scattered somewhere back on the trail. No one said a word about the half-tree the girls decorated that Christmas. Dad made sure of that, feeling bad that we might not have gotten home at all that Christmas.

During the same Christmas break, I saw an example of my mother's kindness— which still often comes to mind. At the height of a raging blizzard, an old man came to our door, selling sewing needles. It was one of those awful nights when the wind howls louder than a passing train and the snow has no chance of ever settling upon the ground. Mama answered the door and greeted the stranger as if he were a long-lost relative returning home. "I'm really sorry," she explained, "but I have no money until Thursday, if you could come back." And then, no surprise to the rest of us, she invited him in from the cold to have supper with the family.

"I'd love a hot meal, Ma'am," he answered, "but, if you don't mind, I'll take it out back there in the tool shed." He left with a cup of hot tea, homemade bread, and a full course meal, fit for a king. "Thank you, Ma'am," he replied softly, and that was all we saw of the stranger. It was not until the spring thaw that anyone had cause to enter the tool shed, and there, neatly stacked along the back wall, were brightly coloured packets of sewing needles: small, medium, and large.

I enjoyed the trip home but by the time it was nearly over I was ready to go back to school in Halifax. I wasn't happy about leaving home, but this time, I knew where I was going and why I needed to be there. I actually looked forward to getting on the train and seeing my new friends.

CHAPTER TWELVE

The first week back at the School after Christmas was almost as lonely as my first time away. It helped that I had friends to play with, but the time that week was long and too much of it spent alone. For a time, I even regretted my decision to return, but that didn't last for long. Back to class with Mrs. Beaton was a welcome distraction: less time to think about home. And, as fortune goes, I met Dr. Samuel Hussey, a totally blind mathematician, teacher, and former Principal at the School, then in his late eighties.

He was tapping his cane on the floor as he passed by and, suddenly, as if he could see, he stopped and spoke to me. "I'm Dr. Hussey," he said, "and what do they call you these days?"

I straightened up and thought, just for a moment, how much he looked like Santa Claus, white beard and all. Right away he invited me to join the School bridge club. The invitation was better than a hug, a timely reminder that this was my family for now and this was my home. Although the bridge club was open to anyone at the School, I still felt handpicked to be there on Friday evenings. It perked me up and off I went, back into school life and thinking less about home.

I enjoyed learning how to play bridge and the freshly made sandwiches served at the break: Cheez Whiz, as I recall. Even more amazing was watching Dr. Hussey and others as they read the Braille cards, remembering practically everything played or dummied on the table. *If he can do things like that with no eyesight,* I thought, *then so what if I can't see the blackboard!* I was proud of him, seeing what I might become someday. I would have taken him to "show and tell" at either of my old schools, but, back in the day, there was no show and tell.

When most blind people were begging on the streets or being sheltered at home, Dr. Hussey was earning his doctorate in Mathematics. And he did it at a time when universities were certainly not welcoming blind students with open arms. I didn't know that when I first met him, or how much he had done to simplify methods for doing Mathematics in Braille, worldwide, or even that he was the Principal of the School some years earlier. And although long retired by the time our paths crossed, he still taught classes in Mathematics and tutored blind students who needed extra help outside the classroom. And he played a mean game of bridge.

I practiced remembering cards with my eyes closed and walking about as if I, too, were totally blind. I did that off and on, trying to see what it was like to see nothing at all. Of course, you never get to see what it's really like; it's too easy to take off the blindfold, and, secondly, as I had noticed months earlier, totally blind people are better at being blind than all the sighted people in the world. As I recall it, walking around blindfolded, tiny steps at a time, with arms extended, was more fearful than instructive.

Another person who made an impression on me in that first year was Mr. Legge, the School Principal. He, too, was partially sighted, seeing better than me at some things and not so much with others.

Principal or not, Mr. Legge couldn't be angry even when you did something wrong two days in a row. He tried to be firm when it was called for, but it usually came out as "Go on now, get out of here before I change my mind." If ever there was a Principal so gentle, it was he, and, to his credit, he kept telling me how smart I was for Grade Three. It was one thing to be complimented, but coming from the Principal, it was double strength. *Imagine that,* I thought, *me, the smart one in Grade Three.* I was never smart before that.

I also saw Mr. Legge, day to day, with the other kids, full of kind words, enthusiasm, and always in a good mood. If he was happy or disappointed with any of us, he'd mutter about it to me or whomever else was in the office, but only in the way a father would talk to one child about another in the family. It was an early kind of breach of privacy, I suppose, but all for the good.

Mr. Legge was quite fond of my friend Tony. They were both from the same region of Newfoundland, but that was only part of it. Tony was full of mischief and famous in our class for getting into trouble. He was sent to the Principal's office as often as I went there for school supplies. When he looked at Tony, I suspect he saw himself as he was when he, too, was a pupil at the School some decades earlier. I recall him saying to me once, "I don't know what I'm to do with that boy!" and he said it with a smile. One of the girls at the School told me, just recently, that Mr. Legge was the father she never had. A lot of that fathering was done while Mr. Legge was Principal.

In the later grades he taught chemistry and physics and filled in whenever one of the teachers was absent. I see him now, magnifier in hand, reading a passage, stopping to explain it and back to reading again. If it happened to be a subject he didn't know as well, it was "get out your books and read the next chapter."

My interest in school grew even stronger as the months passed. I still enjoyed Assembly Hall, and, by mid-year, my chair-caning skills were good enough to cane real chairs, the ones brought to the School for repairs. As soon as my work passed inspection, I got five cents for every hole caned in the chair seat, or, in some cases, the chair back as well. Round or oval seats were more difficult to cane than square ones, but still it was five cents a hole.

I was one of the lucky kids, living close enough to Halifax to get home for Easter. It was one day on the train, a few days at home, and a day to get back. Mom, ever practical and often right, considered ten Chocolate Chunk bars to be a better deal than a chocolate bunny. Earl and I got ten bars each, the cost of one bunny and chocolate enough for two.

And then it was back to school to finish Grade Three. We did endless sums, added and subtracted, and, before the year was over, we jumped up to multiplication, division, and fair warning about things ahead, such as equations and algebra. We even studied international trade in Grade Three, snowballs from Canada in exchange for oranges from Florida, or so the lesson went.

In writing class, instead of using the blackboard, Mrs. Beaton would show each student, one after the other, how to form a capital "W" or a small "b," up close enough for each of us to see where the letter started, where it ended up, and how it got there. She wrote the letters in large print, and, for those who couldn't see as well as me, she wrote even larger.

For the totally blind kids and others who couldn't read print, it was practice in the writing and reading of Braille, beginning with the Braille alphabet, numbers, punctuation marks, and then a kind of shorthand: Braille contractions, hundreds and maybe thousands of contractions, the heart and soul of Braille, must be learned for the more common letter groupings such as "er" and "ing," and some for whole words like "for," "with," "before," and "after"—and more after that. I couldn't believe how many combinations were possible in a simple cell of six dots!

Contractions make Braille more practical, space and time wise, than typing or reading words, one letter at a time. Without contractions, Braille is no more practical than today's teenagers trying to speak without acronyms. And even with that, most Braille books in the School library came in multiple volumes and some that filled one or more shelves.

Braille is not an easy skill to learn and it takes a lot of practice. For those who took the time and made it work, it provided a window on the world that they got to open and close by themselves. Not to mention that when it was lights out for most of us, it was reading time, under the covers, for those who could read Braille.

When winter arrived, I found a second-, a fifth-, or maybe a tenth-hand pair of skates from the School supply, and, before long, I was playing hockey or skating to music with older girls who knew how to make the turns and pull you along. The rink was made and groomed by the older boys. Once in a while the local fire department would show up and give it a good flooding. There were times, too, when the firemen would bring a group of us back to the station for what they called "training" on the big fire trucks and "practice" on the fire pole.

When the snow melted it was baseball where the rink was. Anyone could play if they wished, mostly the boys but not only. For those who were totally blind, it was time at the plate, swinging when told to swing. On contact, someone else would run the bases. It didn't take much to change a few rules and it didn't change the game at all.

At the end of the year, there was a closing ceremony in the auditorium. It was all about the kids, from the little ones in Grade Primary to the graduation class. There were small-money prizes for Braille reading and writing, spelling, music appreciation, piano tuning, best overall student and one for every other subject on the curriculum.

I recall my surprise in winning the award for chair-caning that year, and the fear that went with it: standing up to applause, making my way through the rows of seats and then down the centre aisle to accept the envelope, and to shake hands with someone a lot taller than me. No matter your shoes, you could hear every step on those wooden floors.

I went home with real prizes (silver dollars) and a hippopotamus I'd made out of wood. It was a foundation year for me, that first real year at the School. And it was thanks to good people like Mrs. Flynn for taking a stand, to Mr. Wood for a last pull on the rope, and to Mrs. Beaton for showing me that I could learn like everyone else. Once again, suitcases and trunks lined the corridor, and, this time, the best time of the year, everyone got to go home.

CHAPTER THIRTEEN

Summer was far more enjoyable after that first year at the School for the Blind. I was still very shy and withdrawn, although less so on both counts. My interests had mushroomed to include reading, listening to the news, the latest songs, ball games on the radio, and hockey on the TV. I was more "with it," so to speak; less fearful than before; and far more interested in learning.

It was the summer that cousins Michael and John Mercer moved into the apartment attached to the back of our house. For the next few summers we were inseparable: a foursome that redefined the meaning of good fun and mischief. We ran silly experiments and explored every inch of the forest that surrounded us in all directions.

We practically lived in the woods, classifying everything from flowers and trees to snakes, birds, and insects. Earl and John were always finding things that squirmed under rocks—things I didn't like. We ate tiny bananas from the roots of large ferns, made whistles from twigs, stilts for walking taller, cabins in the woods, and every manner of sling shot and wooden cart.

Michael was more a thinker than hands-on, as I remember. He thought outside the box, thoughts and ideas that made me think as well. He and I put up with the snakes and insects—he less bothered than me— but we were much more interested in what mischief might be lurking around the next corner, like smoking cigarettes and talking about girls.

I'm sure John was a scientist from the very moment of conception. He knew so much about stuff I hadn't even heard of, and, before long, I was interested in science, too.

My brother Earl was the most practical one in the group. He knew what ferns hid bananas in their roots, what berries to pick for making tea, the newest blueberry patches, and where to fish. He baited my hooks and, if you needed someone to build something so that others would come, Earl could do it. He did more for me than a twin brother, helping me to fit in and keep up.

I recall being somewhat of a pest in those days, always falling behind and hollering for them to wait up. But we had lots of fun, camping out, picking crab apples, painting snakes, pouring Kool Aid into a well or making bottle bombs (little ones) by mixing baking soda with liquids and shaking it up.

In all of our time together, I hardly ever mentioned the School for the Blind, people I knew there, or all the things we did. It was that different from home—or so I thought. When at the School, I seldom ever mentioned home. It was like growing up in two different worlds, planets on opposite sides of the same sun.

Once in a while Earl and I would walk with Dad to the nearest lake to fish. Along the way, Dad would show us what wild plants to eat in case we were ever lost; berries to use for tea and what flies were best for fishing this or that lake. I don't think he ever mentioned being a kid or anything about himself, and, of course, we didn't ask either.

At the lake, Dad would wade out by himself and disappear into the cool mist, leaving us to fish off the rocks with a tree branch and a string. For Dad it was trout only; for us it was just little fish with whiskers: catfish, hardly bigger than a popsicle. But there was always that chance-in-one that a trout would pass by and take the worm, mostly Earl's. Dad was usually gone forever and seldom returned without a basket of big fish, never quite like the ones that got away.

All to say that, at home, being visually impaired was a nuisance for sure but it wasn't the problem that people made it out to be. If I did only what other people thought to be possible or safe for someone with poor eyesight in those days, I would have hardly left the house.

We'd often take what food we could carry, just to see how long we could survive in the woods on our own. The record was three days. Mom might have been a little overprotective at times, but she was brave to let me go. She worried, I'm sure, but she let me go, nonetheless. It made me feel more like the other kids.

One day that summer, or maybe the next, Earl and I won a carton of cigarettes on a punch board at the corner store, ten packages with twenty smokes in each. We paid a dime to punch one of the perforations on the board and, bingo, the number matched and the cigarettes were ours. No one cared that we were underage, if, in fact, there was such a thing as being underage in those days. It was enough cigarettes for a daily trip into the woods for most of the summer and a lot of fooling around, dizziness and all.

And there was that time, a few summers later, when Dad came by himself to pick me up at the train station. Mom had just given birth to the last ball player,

Darlene. In the taxi on the way to the hospital, Dad leaned over and offered me a cigarette. It was not my first cigarette, but still, an offer like that from Dad was a coming of age, and, with it, no more smoking behind the barn.

"Don't tell your mother about the cigarette," Dad whispered as we got on the elevator. And those few words I took to be ours, like a secret pact, and somehow I felt a bit more grown up, all of a sudden and all of thirteen.

CHAPTER FOURTEEN

When back at school for Grade Four, I was sad again to leave home but excited to see kids I knew from the previous year and new ones as well. Tony was back and as high-spirited as ever. He was always more grown up and seasoned than me, but not knowing anything about his home or family, I didn't know why. Gary was back, too, and just as interested in cars.

I tried a few times to comfort the younger ones who were homesick and wondering if there really was a Santa Claus. That was common practice, one boy helping another, but, in the end, it was everyone's own mountain to climb. For the smaller ones who spoke French and no English, mostly from northern New Brunswick, it must have been nearly unbearable at times. Nevertheless, they, too, learned to manage.

My Grade Four class was three or four students larger than Grade Three. We sat at tables arranged in a square with the teacher up front. Under the table at each seat was a desk for books and such. I can't remember all of it like it was yesterday, but I do recall Miss or Mrs. Watson, a totally blind teacher, reading us a book in Braille about the circus and what went on behind the scenes. She couldn't have read better or with more expression. I enjoyed watching her read almost as much I enjoyed hearing about the circus.

On one of those visits to the circus, Tony was sneaking around the room, thinking that Miss or Mrs. couldn't see him. He was right about that, but she could hear, and out came the leather strap. Afterwards, she went out into the hall and cried. I felt sorrier for her than for poor Tony who was red in the face and acting like it didn't even hurt. Tony was like that and I admired him for not doing everything he was told. It wouldn't have been me.

I remember struggling with spelling that year because, although I could read print, I saw only the words and seldom looked closer to notice the individual letters. Spelling words exactly as they sound is just asking for mistakes, especially in English.

There was always someone around to help us with a math problem, a bout of sickness, or a loose tooth. We didn't have to walk to school each day, and when it stormed it wasn't us who couldn't get to school, it was the teachers and some of the staff. Once that year, there was no school for two full days and the snow was so deep that we could jump to the ground from two storeys up, either out the windows or off the fire escapes, when nobody was looking.

I didn't feel spoiled at the time, but we did have it pretty good: school just down the corridor, great teachers, good food—lots of it—and good friends. On the other hand, there were no tooth fairies, lullabies, or hugs before bedtime—at least not on the boys' side.

Academically, the School was on a par with the public schools and, with small classes like ours, it was not that difficult to keep up. Lessons followed the Nova Scotia curriculum, but with all kinds of interesting add-ons to fill ten periods a day and five extra ones on Saturday.

It was a heavy schedule, but, in the end, we were all the better for it. Most of the kids who reached Grade Eleven, the final year offered at the School, were as qualified to write provincial exams as any other high-school students from outside.

Evenings were taken up with study periods in the school building or physical fitness in the gym, depending on which day it was. The study periods from 7 to 9 p.m. were not strictly supervised, and there was no requirement to be there if, for some unexplainable reason, you preferred to stay in the TV room to watch *Star Trek*, or, later on, the Beatles on the *Ed Sullivan Show*.

When I was a few years older, the evening study periods provided one more chance to meet the girl who most wanted to meet up with you. An innocent tryst, a minute together, here or there, was enough to make the whole day worthwhile—and more when sealed with a kiss.

The exercise classes, or "drill" as they were called, were not as voluntary. The routine was rigorous but only to the point of what each student could manage, some kids being more disabled than others. You did what you could, and afterwards there was free time in the gym for playing sports or just standing around.

We played volleyball, soccer, and sometimes baseball with a basketball. It was easier to see when at the plate, but six stitches near my left eye, sewn by a kind doctor at the VG Hospital, taught me never to take a full swing at a basketball with a baseball bat. The back-at-you-effect was no picnic. But, if you must, make sure never to hit the ball flush in the middle.

As to soccer, no one ever got in John Stroud's way when he'd wind up to kick the ball. John was totally blind and stronger than anyone at the School. It was usually a totally blind kid in the net with the rest of us hollering for the ball.

After gym class it was free time until bedtime, and for me, now in Grade Four, that was 9 o'clock, a full half-hour later than in Grade Three, and one more dorm down the hall.

Each year, new students arrived and others left and it wasn't long before I knew most of the kids around my own age. I knew how well or poorly they could see and where everyone came from; seems we all knew those two things about each other. We were almost proud to say where we came from. I know I was and I think I know why: it was your home.

I hardly remember anyone at school without at least one friend, and even with eighty boys living in the same house, there were few fights that I know of, mostly squabbles and endless bouts of wrestling.

I met a lot of the girls as well, and knew many of them by name; the teachers, too, and most of the staff. It was one large family away from home. I never thought of it exactly that way in Grade Four, but I see it that way now.

One afternoon, an older boy fainted in the washroom and I helped him to his feet with another boy. I recall being rather impressed that he asked to see both of us the next day, like an older brother, just to say thank you and remark that if we didn't help each other, we may as well go home.

Not long before my arrival at the School, a high metal fence in the back yard, separating the boys from the girls, was taken down. It was the Sixties, the decade to change the world, free love and all. The School was trying to keep up, and when it got there, we were expected to behave accordingly. And we must have done a good job of it because, to my knowledge, there were no serious violations of any kind, save a few stolen kisses and a few made-up stories, mostly from the boys. The stories were innocent enough, although spiced with a pinch of exaggeration. I'm told that after the fence came down, the boys combed their hair before going out and the girls, too, big hair and all.

CHAPTER FIFTEEN

Grade Four was in the books and there were piles of new books for Grade Five, more work, and less time for fooling around. Two new students arrived in my class that year: Tommy Anstey and Monte Single, both from Newfoundland and both to become good friends of mine, right up to graduation in Grade Eleven.

I looked around for Tony whom I had known since Grade Three, but when classes resumed, he wasn't there. I assumed he had just stayed home but, sadly, that was not the case. Poor Tony had passed away that summer on a construction site. "What the devil was he doing there?" Mr. Legge would ask, over and over again.

The School had three mechanical models of the solar system (orreries) that I particularly liked. How they ever stayed together, turning nine orbits at different speeds at the same time, I don't know. Playing with them got me interested in astronomy. In Grade Five I seldom left the Public Library downtown without a new planet to visit or star charts to study.

In the classrooms there were tactile maps, embossed diagrams, models like those of the solar system, and a large print encyclopedia. In the library, a large collection of books in Braille and some in raised letters filled the shelves. Popular games like checkers and chess, cards and bingo were provided in the TV room, most of them modified slightly to accommodate those with poor vision or no vision at all: bingo and playing cards in Braille and large print, chess pieces that locked in until moved again, tactile puzzles, many things to keep us amused.

I was fond of radios, especially the old tube ones you could take apart. After I watched Chris Stark skipping around the world on his ham radio set, he suggested I take the course offered by volunteers from outside the School. I didn't work at it hard enough to tap the sixty words per minute as required by Mr. Morse, so I lost interest.

Instead, I went about making crystal radios with a wire coil, a nail, a metal clip, and earphones. The radio could be attached to a radiator or any of the water pipes that wormed about the School. I learned that the pipes carried radio waves. The crystal set had its own special sound, high-pitched and hollow as if coming in from outer space or at least from a long distance away. It was a far cry from a ham radio set or the radio my grandmother gave me.

By Grade Five, poor vision aside, I set my sights on becoming a professional baseball pitcher. *Why not*, I thought, *I really like baseball!* I spent months outside, throwing a ball as hard as I could, way up and against the red bricks of the school building. From that I got a sore shoulder and a rubber arm, for a time, but to me that was just part of the training.

By Grade Six I hadn't yet given up a future in baseball and, strangely, I wasn't even that good at it. I tired myself out for days throwing a hard softball up and against the plastered ceiling in my dorm. One afternoon when, thankfully, we were all in class, half the ceiling collapsed onto the beds. It was a high ceiling and the mess of white dust and huge chunks of plaster, on and between the beds, looked like serious trouble to me, enough to be expelled.

I had no idea that a softball—which is much harder than it sounds—could do that kind of damage. Still, I knew it was my fault and, fearing the worst, I wasn't about to fess up. I didn't even mention it at Saturday Confession; you never knew who was listening.

I can only imagine what was done at the School to

make sure that didn't happen again. And if it did, it wasn't going to be because of me. Seeing that ceiling on the floor shattered all dreams of playing baseball for money. Instead, I decided to become a millionaire.

Outside the School, I was one of the regulars to walk the paths and feed the ducks at the Public Gardens. I often went to the Halifax Public Library to borrow books, to the Nova Scotia Museum, and, later on, to movies at the Capitol Theatre. I knew every store on Spring Garden Road, down to Barrington Street and left or right from there.

One day I found a book at the Public Library, *One Thousand Free Things to Order by Mail*—or it might have been ten thousand, I'm not sure. For as long as I had money for stamps, I got more mail than anyone else at the School: miniature bars from Neilson, maps from the government, pins, stickers, cut-outs, pamphlets, and coupons for things I'd never think to buy.

One of my teachers, noting my affinity for mail, gave me an article from a magazine about a man who painted pictures of the little ponies on Sable Island. I wrote to him as the teacher suggested and one day I got a letter back with a dozen or more sketches of ponies, standing up, lying down, or running on the sand. I showed them to everyone at school.

For a time, I ran the boys' canteen, refilled the pop machines, and, for fifty cents a meal, I served tables at dinner time in the Juniors' dining room. The little kids were more than polite and more so than the older ones, never forgetting to say "please" and "thank you." They were always clean and well-dressed, a credit to the staff on the Juniors' side, although I wouldn't have thought like that back then.

I learned plenty from those odd jobs at the School, but mostly it was the awful smell of scraping plates into the slop pail that got me thinking about becoming a millionaire.

But I didn't think about money all the time. We had a school newspaper, *The HSB Maritimes*, and someone wrote in, suggesting record hops on weekends. From then on there were record hops, although not every weekend. I remember my first one, dancing with Nina, the girl who came over and talked to me the first day in Grade Three. I'm sure it was she who asked me to dance; I would have been too shy to make the first move—or even the second.

Around that time, one of the radio stations in Halifax donated a few thousand old records, mostly 78s made of breakable Bakelite; perhaps they'd heard about the record hops. The donated records were piled in one of the rooms on the music floor; the pile reached almost to the ceiling. We could rummage through the pile and keep anything we wanted.

More than a few evenings were spent in that room,

trying one record after another. As most of the records were of pre-war vintage, there wasn't much we wanted. In fact, we never found one you'd dare play at the record hop. When all were auditioned, only one survived: "The Old Grey Mare, She Ain't What She Used to Be," and that, only because it was more funny than musical. I've often wondered who ended up cleaning the mess we left behind in that room.

We were also fortunate that the School understood the wisdom of employing older blind students to supervise the younger ones. The first of those students in my time at the School was Emery Leblanc. He dressed like it was always Sunday and never passed us by without stopping to say hello. He took an interest in what we were doing at school and, being a student himself, he knew what to ask and what to say. It was people like Emery and, later on, other supervisors like Cleon Smith and Gilbert Murray who filled in as a father, a counsellor, or an older brother.

Emery left the School a few years later and joined the Canadian National Institute for the Blind. He was sent to Sydney, my home town, to replace Mr. Wood who was soon to take a new position in Halifax. It was the same Mr. Wood who talked my mother into sending me to school in Halifax.

Sadly, Mr. Wood, one of his sons, and Emery as well were drowned in a tragic boating accident, not long after and not very far from shore. When I heard the terrible news, I was home in Sydney for summer holidays, but for a time my thoughts were back at the School with Emery and the other kids.

It may have been Emery, I'm not sure, but someone put me down for rink duty in Grade Six. Flooding was best done late at night and once, when it was double-digits below zero, we were up 'til four in the morning. We accomplished the first flooding with a firehose given to the School by the local fire department.

One night, Tommy and I and another good friend, Melvin MacNeil, went inside for one of the perks of rink duty: hot chocolate and sandwiches from the kitchen. We left the hose outside and it froze solid. We bent it enough to get it inside and under the hot showers in the gym. It took a full hour of steam to thaw it out and another hour of flooding before the night shift was done.

Having been up most of the night nursing a hose, I faked a toothache next morning and didn't get to class until after lunch. I thought I got away with it! Two weeks later, however, I found myself lined up with another dozen kids, and off we went to the Dalhousie Dental School. They must have liked me there because they invited me back, one week after another. It was hours upon hours of dental students inside my mouth, learning their way and making their teacher proud.

When all was drilled and plyers set at rest, four of my upper front teeth were gone forever, along with one big molar from each side, for balance, I suppose. In return, I got suckers, a partial plate, and nightmares of going to dental school.

The School for the Blind was a magnet for celebrities visiting Halifax. I got to meet and shake hands with real hockey players from Hockey Night in Canada, players like Ted Lindsay, Peter Mahovlich, Dick Harvey, and Dicky Duff, too, when he was out on crutches. I also met Jack Dempsey, one of the greatest boxers of all time. As he had already retired before I was born—or almost—he was just a kindly man to me with a hand-shake as big as a hug.

And, of course, being that young, we never missed watching weekly wrestling from Maple Leaf Gardens, huddling around the TV, yelling and cheering as the good ones won and the bad ones lost. You could almost tell who would win or lose by how they looked and how they behaved before the match.

One weekend, I suppose it was during the off-season, the full cast from Maple Leaf Gardens came for a visit at the School. I couldn't believe it but there we all were, down in the school gymnasium, wrestling with Whipper Billy Watson, Bulldog Brower, the Kalmikoff Brothers, and even the crowd favourite, Tony Marino.

The mats were on the floor and so were we, wrestling with heroes. I was disappointed, though, because they didn't really hate each other like on television. The older boys said it was all fake, more of an acrobatic show than a real wrestling match. After that, I lost interest and moved on and up a notch to boxing.

CHAPTER SIXTEEN

I could see, very early on, that blindness included kids who were totally blind, those who could see only light and shadows, and others, like me, with partial sight.

The partially sighted kids formed the largest group at the School by far. In this group, even those of us with the same eye condition might see the world in very different ways. Most of us could see the big "E" on the doctor's eye chart, but nothing more, giving us the same acuity score on paper, and yet, what we saw was not the same. I could read and write print, as an example, while others couldn't. Some could play baseball in the daylight and others only at dusk. Others could do fine needlework, while another could hardly catch a basketball.

Explaining what partially sighted people actually see gets even more fuzzy when you add into the equation varying degrees of colour perception, blurriness, light sensitivity, or restricted fields of vision. You get the picture, but even then, with so many variables, you don't really. It's as hard to pin down as it is for me to imagine what it's like to see 20/20.

I've seen more ophthalmologists in my lifetime than eye drops in a bottle, and, despite the obvious limitations of the eye chart, not one has ever taken the time to ask what I "actually" see. One of the least attentive, a man in a blue shirt and a bright red tie, insisted that I couldn't possibly see colour. I'm not supposed to have depth perception either, having vision in only one eye, but I know I do. I can't prove it, and science says it's not possible, but in my mind's eye, I see it every day: a world of curves and crevices, roundness and fullness.

Despite the ranting, I'd be first in line to say that ophthalmologists make miracles come true every day— and twice in my own case. The first happened when the retina in my one good eye totally detached and the second when the same doctor returned me to partial sight after a surgery-induced cataract. But still, blind and visually impaired people expect that if there's anyone out there who knows what they actually see or don't see, it must be their ophthalmologist.

For every cause of blindness, there was someone at the School to raise its banner. There were kids with congenital disorders of all kinds, and others blinded from infection or diseases like scarlet fever, meningitis, and diabetes. Some of the kids were blind from accidents and far too many from human error, as in too much oxygen during incubation or deformities of all kind from drugs like thalidomide. The sound of that word, even today, is cringe inducing.

No matter how limited some of the kids were, particularly when mental and other physical disabilities got added to blindness, they found friends like themselves and laughed as often as I did. It was no different than people of the same culture coming together, speaking the same language, getting the same jokes or bearing the same burdens. Whether adding sums in the classroom, playing music, or kicking a ball, they participated as best they could, and much better there than in public schools as they were, back then, in the early Sixties.

There were some kids, I'm sure, who needed more attention and more advanced support than what the School provided, but, overall, you'd be amazed at what these kids accomplished. I learned so much from just watching and listening. As young boys we sometimes teased the ones who had the higher mountains to climb. In that sense, regrettably, we were no different than other kids.

As many kinds of blindness are hereditary, there were lots of brothers and sisters attending the School.

I envied them, thinking selfishly how nice it would be if Earl were there or an older sister to watch over me. Despite the rules and close supervision for keeping the boys and the girls apart, brothers and sisters were allowed to meet and spend time together.

For the blind children with mental and other related learning disabilities, the School offered auxiliary classes with a slowed-down curriculum. There, the kids could work at their own pace with other students like them, talking, laughing, and learning at nearly the same pace.

For the more severely disabled children—and there were many at the School—blindness was sometimes the lesser of ills. I used to think a large team of social workers and psychologists might have helped, but a good friend from the School, Vivian Maclean, reminded me recently of how much these kids did for themselves. When I thought of how they came together and all the things they did, I saw what she meant.

As to behaviour, the kids at the school were no less full of mischief nor better behaved than anywhere else. I heard and repeated my share of bad words and off-colour jokes, having such a large group of friends to draw upon and older boys who were generous enough to share.

If by some stroke of luck a door was left unlocked or a classroom unsupervised, we were sure to take full advantage. When old enough to know better, thirteen or fourteen, we often played with the mineral rocks and chemicals that filled the chemistry cabinet in one of the classrooms. The cabinet was often left unlocked and unattended.

We played with droplets of mercury, sulfuric acid, ammonia, and other chemicals that should have been locked away. One of those chemicals got mixed into a bottle of pop and passed around the school. I didn't drink the pop, but there was such a commotion about it, something important going on, that not wanting to be left out, I joined in and said I did.

Within the hour a dozen of us were lined up and rushed to the VG Hospital across the street. All stomachs were disgustingly pumped and lesson learned. I didn't need to be there, but on the plus side, after swallowing a plastic tube and throwing up whatever had gone down, we got ice cream and had to drink enough cold milk to frighten a cow. I wouldn't recommend it, but the feeling of ice cream and cold milk on an entirely empty stomach was absolutely heavenly. However, getting there was no fun.

I wouldn't have been alone in faking a cold or a sore throat either, the nursing station being such a pleasant place where Aspergum and kind words were given out like candy. It seemed, at the time, that Aspergum was the cure for everything. In times of extended illness, you got to sleep over in the medical ward. It was a nice rest from the daily routine of school and lineups. It was breakfast in bed, a private nurse, or so it seemed, a bath and clean sheets every day. Overall, with about 180 boys and girls living at the school, we were well cared for.

CHAPTER SEVENTEEN

If it wasn't for the fact that, back then, the Halifax School for the Blind was only one hundred years old, you might think music was invented there—it was that much a part of every day. I wasn't gifted myself on that scale, but I loved music.

The sight and sound of the brass pipe organ in the auditorium was as much an integral part of the old School as a violin is to an orchestra, and we were fortunate to hear it, almost daily. We heard it sometimes at morning assembly, sometimes when students were practicing, and often at recitals.

I didn't know and probably wouldn't have found it all that interesting at the time, but the organ was built by the famous Casavant Frères in Saint-Hyacinthe, Quebec. It was hand-delivered in 1913 and installed at the back of the stage, in an alcove set aside for that purpose by Sir Frederick Fraser, the first School superintendent.

The organ was useful for training blind people for employment, mostly in churches, but it was also a source of music and delight for all of us, including the Halifax Symphony Orchestra that came there to practice from time to time. When they did, we were sometimes invited to listen in.

At one practice, the conductor mentioned a young boy in the audience who was particularly fond of Handel's Water Music, and that happened to be me. He asked me to stand and take a bow, after which the orchestra played the second movement, the only one I actually didn't like. Of course, I didn't say so, especially to Miss Hubley, the Head of the Music Department, and the one most likely to have singled me out for a bit of attention that afternoon. She was always good to me.

Miss Hubley taught us to appreciate classical music. We studied the great composers, heard their music, and learned the instruments of the orchestra by sound and by name: Newt the Flute, Tony the Tuba, and so on. She played us records and we sat there quietly and listened, more interested in the Beatles but at the same time unaware of how much appreciation of classical music we were absorbing. I still like the Beatles, but give me Mozart anytime.

But that organ! You could actually climb up and into it or down a flight of stairs to a secret room under the stage. I found that room with Tommy Anstey one day and we, along with invited guests from time to time, claimed it as a hideout, a place to be silly and to smoke cigarettes. We thought we had rediscovered a place long forgotten. Rumour was that older students operated a still in that room during the war years, and whether true or not, whether the First or Second World War, it made the room all that more daring.

When I think of music at the School, I think of students like Terry Kelly, a totally blind friend who was no more than five or six years old (me, eleven) when we met for the first time. He was alone in one of the classrooms, typing on a Braille writer. I stopped in to say "hello" just when the bell on the writer sounded to signal the end of a line. "B-flat," Terry announced out loud, like he was being tested. I asked him how he knew it was B flat and he answered me right away, "I just know it." He didn't know, nor did I, that music would become his livelihood or that skill and lots of hard work would, someday, place him in the elite company of the Order of Canada.

Terry wasn't the only one at the School with perfect pitch. We all knew Mary Whiffen, a totally blind girl from Newfoundland. Every morning at Assembly Hall she played the piano on stage and sometimes she played the big pipe organ, always from memory. Before Mr. Allen would take the stage, she'd played just for us. If it wasn't "Wheels" or "Greensleeves," it was some other piece from the hit parade. I'm sure Mr. Allen liked it as well because he never walked onto the stage until the piece was over.

Being a few years younger, I didn't know Mary that well, but once, at a school gathering, I braved-up and asked her to play something I had heard on the radio. She smiled and invited me to sit next to her on the piano bench while she played. I felt I knew her after that, seeing her every day on stage, at school recitals and at the end of the year, winning more prizes for achievement than anyone else. If there was a prize for winning the most prizes or making us smile, it belonged to Mary. She was better than very good at almost everything from music to Braille reading, Braille writing and first in her class as well.

Sadly, Mary passed away in an apartment fire a few years after leaving the School. I was bothered enough when hearing the bad news to look up and ask why. But there was no answer; how could there be?

And who can forget Jimmy Noseworthy playing the piano in the Smoker? I hardly ever smoked a cigarette there without listening to Jimmy playing whatever was current on the hit parade. If you requested a piece he hadn't heard, you'd hum it and he'd pick it up right away. If he wanted a voice as tuneful as his own, there was Dennis McCormack nearby with a guitar to join in. And there was Justin Hull standing near the wall, talking with Martin Daley or Ed Russell. And no doubt Ed was relating the latest current events he'd heard about on the CBC, never without commentary, and never without a laugh. Ed had the quickest wit I've ever heard, then or since.

I can still hear Emile Haché playing Acadian tunes on the mouth organ down in the basement, talking and laughing in between jigs, with Robert Just and David Beard. David played the accordion the way it was played in Newfoundland. There was a lot of music around but, surprisingly, no fiddle. You'd think someone would have played the fiddle at the School, considering the number of kids from Acadian New Brunswick or Scottish Cape Breton, but there were none that I remember.

Whether Fred Haines on the banjo, Rodrick Richard on the guitar, or Michael Kilburn learning to play his new guitar, it all sounded wonderful to me. There was always someone playing music somewhere at the School, kids I envied and looked up to at the same time.

I looked up to Susan Small, a blind concert pianist who played for us on stage, sometimes at Assembly Hall and other times at school recitals. She wouldn't have known, but listening to her playing Beethoven or Mozart, all from memory, got me interested in classical music.

From time to time recitals were held in the auditorium for students and invited guests from outside the School. And like so many of the kids, I, too, was enrolled in piano lessons and more than once called up to perform on stage.

I got paired up at one recital to play a piano duet with my friend, Tommy. We, two thirteen-year-olds, practiced that piece for months, but when on stage with the auditorium filled, I lost my way right at the start, leaving poor Tommy playing nothing but the bass notes. Miss Hubley was quick to her feet, "Boys, boys, let's try that again, please!" We tried it once more, but this time it was Tommy who messed up. "That'll be all for now," Miss Hubley decided with a loud clap of her hands, and back we went to our seats, red in the face and giggling quietly to ourselves.

A few concerts later and it was my turn again, solo this time, to play the "The Mouse in the Coal Bin" by Charles Peerson. I played the notes softly and slowly, climbing higher and higher up the keyboard as I was taught (the mouse climbing the lumps of coal). When nearly at the top, a loud and rapid pounding on the keys tells of the mouse falling all the way down to start slowly back up again.

I practiced that piece for months and never once

thought it funny until I played it on stage that evening. When the mouse climbed, the audience was dead quiet and when it fell back down, they laughed out loud. I couldn't help laughing as well, but somehow I managed to finish the piece, all the notes in the right place. For my reward, I felt the rush of loud applause. It was not a standing ovation as it would have been for Susan Small or Ann Masterton, but I was still proud of myself!

I didn't know at the time but those moments on stage, the hours of practice and the music itself, were powerful tools for building confidence and character. I wasn't instantly less shy and withdrawn as a result, but I'm sure it helped, one melody at a time.

And, finally, there was that wonderful Grandfather clock that sounded the chimes of Westminster while standing guard at the entrance to the girls' residence. It chimed away the hours in my head for nine years and if ever it stopped while I was there, I didn't hear it.

CHAPTER EIGHTEEN

By the time I was in Grade Seven, a core group of us ended up in the same class and stayed together until graduation. There was Monte Single and Tommy Anstey from Grade Five, Melvin MacNeil who arrived in Grade Six, and then Michael Kilburn who joined the set in Grade Seven. Monte was the only Braille student in the group; the rest of us saw well enough to read print. And Monte was better than most Braille students, always winning this or that prize for Braille reading and writing.

It was Monte who first told me about the annual car rally through the streets of Halifax for totally blind students from the School. As I recall hearing, there were numerous teams of two, a sighted driver and a blind student. The blind student gave directions to the driver from instructions and clues written in Braille. The object: first to the finish line.

The five of us grew up and learned together like brothers in any family. We didn't always get along but most times we did, and when we didn't, it was just boys being boys, competing, wrestling, and being silly.

Tommy kept us laughing most of the time. Michael had all the Beatles records, while Monte and Melvin, in their quiet unassuming manner, added good sense and balance along the way. And me, I was too serious back then, always studying like I had to come first. I suppose that, too, had something to do with how it felt when I showed up last at everything in public school. On the plus side, I was passionate about learning and never once showed up for school, or later on for work, without my homework done.

As a group, we were fortunate to end up in the same class, year after year. We were singled out at school and Misters Brooks, Nickerson, and Legge, and Mrs. McClusky, did their best to mold young minds for later release into the "wide and wicked world," or so they called it. Whether the world was really wide and wicked, the term was often used to remind us that being blind at the School was a lot easier than being blind outside in a sighted world.

As a class, we were studious enough, but, at the same time, we were kids, teenagers looking to be noticed, living and dying on every breath, like the world would end if you got a bad haircut. And speaking of hair, poor

Tommy's was so curly, wiry, and closely cropped that no one passed him by without rubbing his head. You'd think, at least once, he'd be annoyed. But not Tommy; he was always in a good mood.

Romances at the School were as commonplace as flowers in May. If couples weren't walking the path around the perimeter of the schoolyard, they were sneaking a kiss between classes or holding hands while skating on the school rink. The first hands I held belonged to Valerie Beaulieu from New Brunswick, but she let them go when baseball season came along and took up most of my time.

My first and more serious love arrived at the School when I was in Grade Nine. She hardly spoke a word of English, and me, not a word of French. I started going to early morning Mass during Lent, all forty days, because she was too religious not to be there. I may have let on that I, too, was just as religious as she was but, thank God, it worked. I'm sure it wasn't long before she found me out.

Roseline Boudreau and I held hands and walked along the metal fence in the back yard, past the lilac trees and back again until the end of the year. I was hoping to see her back the next year, but she wasn't there, and apart from meeting on one other occasion, we soon lost touch.

That same year, Tommy and I thought it was time to

try something a bit harder than the Sussex pop in the pop machine. We got a friend, a former student, to get us a bottle of rum, Captain Morgan, I think. On Friday evening we headed out with two other friends for Point Pleasant Park, a safe distance from the School. We sat on the rocks surrounding the duck pond and mixed rum with Mountain Dew, anything to kill the taste.

By the time it was dark, the bottle was almost gone and so were we, laughing and raising hell. Just when the party shifted into third gear, out of the woods came two police officers in full uniform. "Now you boys tone it down," one of them shouted in a gruff voice, "and get your things, you're coming with us!"

The officer turned to me first and asked for my name and address, but not nearly as nicely as Mrs. Beaton had done in Grade Three. I told him we were students at the School for the Blind and that was enough. It was like sprinkling sugar on sour rhubarb as both officers turned instantly nice, friendly enough to let us go home on our own, without the sirens, the flashing lights, or the rest of the bottle.

As good as the food was at the School, we were teenagers, craving a hamburger or just time away from the School premises. And that's why most of us ended up at the Tasty Food Restaurant, a few blocks down Morris Street. I'm sure some of us still know the menu by heart.

The restaurant was like a home away from the School, a place to eat and talk among ourselves; the boys, that is, as the girls at our age were not allowed out. The restaurant was particularly busy on evenings when canned spaghetti or cans of anything were on the School's supper menu.

Being there so often, Tommy and I got smart one day and offered a pick-up and delivery service for kids and staff back at the School. Thereafter, he and I took control of the late-night food trade on the boys' side. We'd make the rounds every evening at about 9 o'clock to take food orders. For a very reasonable ten cents per order, never once increased, food was picked up and delivered, hot and soggy. It was a hot chicken sandwich for Gilbert Murray, fish and chips for Cleon Smith, or a fried egg sandwich for those who couldn't wait for breakfast the next morning. The same professional service would have been offered to the girls and probably for half the price, if we could have snuck past the Grandfather clock or the watchful eyes of the girls' supervisors.

The monopoly went on for years, keeping Tommy and me in cigarettes and pocket money all the way to graduation.

At one of the school dances someone made the mistake of putting Tommy and me in charge of the food. We collected money enough to order 400 hamburgers for pick-up from the Tasty Food restaurant. We could barely carry the box back to the School, and when the dance was over, we could barely believe our eyes either. Almost 200 hamburgers were left over and had to be thrown away. I ordered fish and chips with gravy, after that, for the rest of the year—and maybe all of high school as well.

CHAPTER NINETEEN

Along with High School came the privilege of a semi-private bedroom, a kind of rite of passage at the School, making you more grown-up than the year before. I remember feeling good about having gotten that far, a long way from the second dorm on the first floor in Grade Three and bedtime at 8:30 p.m.

Being twice lucky, my roommate that year was Melvin, the quieter one in the group of five, and just up the hall were Tommy, Monte, and Michael. Melvin had a fondness for music and a turntable for playing LPs and 45s. All the latest records belonging to whomever were turned on that player. Every Sunday, in the Smoker, we'd huddle around the radio to count down the top ten songs on the hit parade.

It was also the time, the mid-sixties, when portable reel-to-reel tape recorders entered the classroom. For blind people, it was a significant breakthrough, providing more access to reading materials and freedom to make choices. Before that, the only available books were either in Braille or pre-recorded books for the blind. But to actually record what you needed, when you needed it, or to rewind it and hear it again: these were big changes for all of us at the School.

Tape recorders, and, soon after that, compact cassettes provided us with hours upon hours of freely recorded music from the radio or from records. It was said to be illegal, but you couldn't arrest the whole world. And there was no shortage of volunteers to read to us, either reading books onto a tape or reading in person.

In Grade Ten I met a new girlfriend as well: Mildred Kelly, from Trinity, Newfoundland. We met on the train back to school that year and, for once, I wasn't taking much notice of all the stops along the way. In fact, the more the better. Mildred could see a little better than me, and for a few years we held hands in the schoolyard and then, a few years later, we got married and raised two wonderful children, Robert Scott and Kelly Ann.

I liked everything about Mildred, but most especially her calm and quiet manner; while me, I was always ranting on about this or that. We're still good friends, no longer together, but for no other reason than having grown apart, me in overdrive and Mildred, still calm and quiet.

At the beginning of Grade Ten, the teachers had the same names as before, names like Brooks, Nickerson, Legge, or McCluskey, but they seemed different that year. Over the summer they had changed into part-time parents, while continuing to work full-time as teachers.

There was less distance between student and teacher, and more discussion in the classroom on stuff beyond the textbooks. Perhaps it was just us who had changed, being more grown-up and capable of making at least some of our own decisions.

There was more freedom as well on the social side, and no end of creative ways to meet up with a girl-friend, either outside or inside the School. Despite the best efforts of mice, and mouse traps to keep the boys and the girls apart, it didn't take much imagination to skirt the rules. For starters, you could meet for a few minutes between classes or during study periods in the evenings.

Although the residences were supervised twenty-four-seven, downstairs in the basement of the old building, where the kitchen separated the boys' and girls' dining rooms, there was clear passage, unguard-ed, from one residence basement to the other. No one would dare go too far inside, but you could arrange to meet in the kitchen, in secret, if only to talk and hold hands. And Joe, the night watchman, would sometimes stand by and keep watch, but only for a few minutes: he had rounds to do and clocks to punch.

Outside the school, most couples met at the Capital Theatre on Barrington Street. Movies didn't change that often in those days, and there was only one theatre nearby, so you'd end up watching the same film with the same girl, or the same film with another girl, over and over again.

We also congregated at the Tasty Food restaurant on Morris Street where Gloria, the waitress, and both George and Louis, the owners, knew all of us by name or the food we ordered. It was *our Happy Days* diner with a jukebox, vinyl booths, arborite tables, and red bar stools at the counter. And the menu was just the same as on television: milkshakes, coke floats, hamburgers, fries, and a big jar of donuts on the counter.

In the following and my final year at the School, Grade Eleven, we worked just as hard. Mr. Brooks always wanted to teach Latin and we thought we always wanted to learn it. We tried it for a while until we got tired of learning what Mr. Brooks got tired of teaching.

Mr. Nickerson let me teach part of the Grade Eleven course in geometry as I knew more of it than he did. He was the English teacher, filling in for someone else, and I was gifted in mathematics. By the time provincial exams rolled around, we were all ready.

The closing ceremonies and graduation dance marked the end of my time at the School for the Blind in Halifax. I was brought there in 1958 by my parents, and to see them back for the closing ceremonies in 1967 was a fitting way to bring it to a close. Dad, who loved music as much as I did, was impressed to see me in the School choir. He didn't know that, for years, I mimed the words, having no voice as nice as those around me.

I was proud to have my parents there to see, first-hand, how right they were to have brought me there in the first place. I was proud as well to win the Math Cup named in memory of Dr. Hussey, the man who had invited me to join the bridge club in Grade Three.

When my parents left the following day, I stayed over for another week to write provincial exams and, from there, it was out and into the so-called "wide and wicked" world. Some of us remained in Halifax for a few years after graduation but, eventually, as life goes, we ended up in different parts of the country. Immediately after the School, I attended Saint Mary's University, and I'm baffled, even today, when recalling that, back then, I had no idea that going to university—unlike the School for the Blind—cost money. It wasn't ever mentioned at home or at the School. On registration day, I was asked for $700 to cover tuition and $3,000 for room and board. I had no money except a $200 scholarship from the School for the Blind.

I picked up the phone and called the office of Percy Gaum, the Minister of Welfare for Nova Scotia. I politely asked his secretary for an appointment, not for the next month but for that very afternoon.

"I'm sorry," she said kindly, "but the Minister is far too busy. What's it about, perhaps someone else can help you."

"No," I replied, "I need to see the Minister. It's personal and it's urgent." Without an appointment for that day or even that month, I walked a few miles down to see him anyway. After all, he was from Sydney, my hometown.

When I got there, the secretary was surprised to see me, but nice about it as well. "I'm sorry again," she said, "but the Minister will not be able to see you. His schedule is fully booked." I didn't really think that anyone was that busy, or that people stayed in the office all night long, so I sat there and waited.

In all of ten minutes, the door opened and there was Mr. Gaum, the Minister. "So, who do we have here?" he asked the secretary. Something got murmured and before I could get up and introduce myself, the Minister came over and shook my hand. "Come in and sit down," he insisted, and then he listened to me explain the mess

I was in. "Well, let's see what we can do about that," he said, like he had already solved the problem. Two senior officials came into the office and, no kidding, the conversation went like this:

"Now listen," the Minister began, "this young man is a busy student here at Saint Mary's, so let's not hold him up. He's a graduate of the School for the Blind and needs money for university. Let's get his tuition and meal ticket paid and do you smoke?" he asked me.

"Yes," I said timidly, as if no one else smoked in those days.

"Then let's make sure he has a bit of pocket money as well," added the Minister. And just like that, the university got paid, cigarettes got smoked, and I graduated with honours three years later.

I was pleased to awaken a source of funding for higher education of persons with disabilities. It was there all along, but not used or at least not publicized. I was doubly pleased to spread the news to other blind people interested in studies after high school. In those days it was almost impossible for blind or visually impaired students to work part-time while in school, or to find a summer job to earn their own way.

Regretfully, I never saw Minister Gaum after that, and I never thought to look him up in later years to say a proper "thank you." Some years later, as luck would have it, I met the former Minister's nephew in Ottawa and passed along the story of a good man I had once met in downtown Halifax.

I didn't know what confidence was all about at the age of ten, when first arriving at the School. But by the time I graduated in 1967, I had as much confidence as Canada had that year, when celebrating its first Centennial birthday. Even with that, I had no idea of what exactly I wanted to do, beyond going to university and being there to study. Study what—I figured to find that out when I got there.

And yes, as we were warned, the world outside was bigger than the School, and at times there were hills to climb that shouldn't have been there, but so it is for most everyone with a disability.

At the time, Saint Mary's University was well ahead of the world in accommodating students with disabilities. I recall meeting with one of the Jesuits to ask for extra time to write the final exam; I couldn't possibly finish a two-hour written exam in the same time as students with full sight. We chatted for a while and it wasn't long before the conversation turned to the many topics covered during the course that term. "Well," he said at the end of our conversation, "you're not a philosopher yet, but you certainly know Philosophy 101." He gave me a pass mark and told me not to bother writing the exam.

I liked working with numbers and thought I might

be an accountant. But after two months of student employment in an audit firm, struggling with handwritten numbers in awkward-to-hold ledgers, a good-hearted supervisor gave me some useful feedback: "Robert," he said, "you know as much as I do about accounting principles, but, my God, you're slow!" It was honest feedback of the rarest kind, but kind no less. I remained at Saint Mary's, but I changed my major to Economics instead. Upon graduation, I moved on to Law School at Dalhousie University.

Having left the School for the Blind with a sound academic foundation, I had no problem in earning a degree, making my way into the Jesuit Honours Society, or even qualifying for Law School. It was Mrs. Beaton and my high-school teachers who paved the way for that, encouraging me to go beyond the curriculum.

At university, I lived as a partially blind person in a sighted world. At the School for the Blind, I was partially sighted, and going from one to the other, the School to university, was a difficult transition at first. It was the little things that caused me the most angst, like finding a seat in a classroom, or getting there on time, or serving myself in the cafeteria, and, worst of all, not recognizing people I'd already met. I saw facial outlines, but not well enough to tell an aquiline nose from a pudgy one, or a round pumpkin face from a square one.

Eventually I learned to recognize some people by what they wore, and, although not foolproof, it was still a useful clue. Of course, people don't always wear the same clothes, but you'd be surprised how similarly a certain person dresses from one day to the next. Most of the other students at university had no idea how poor my vision was, and that was my fault for not saying so—as if trying to pass for someone with good eyesight was *that* important. It wasn't that I was embarrassed about being visually impaired; I was mostly over that. But I was young and super sensitive about silly things, like appearing to be the same as everyone else. Also, wherever I looked, I saw mostly obstacles in the paths of people with disabilities, barriers created mostly by misunderstanding. So, I wasn't about to put it out there, to say I was visually impaired every time I met someone, unless I had to.

In hindsight, I should have carried a white cane as I now do, seldom leaving home without it. But, when young, you want desperately to be like everyone else, even though I wasn't like everyone else, not really. Regardless, it would have been so much easier with a white cane to show people that, once in a while, I could use a little help. I got good at asking for help when needed, and I didn't come to see the sense of carrying a white cane until after I retired. In that regard, a totally blind person has some small advantage over someone with partial sight, because they get noticed, and, in most cases, by people wanting to lend a helping hand.

I think of my friend Vivian from the School who tells of crossing a busy street in downtown Toronto with a white cane in her hand and an infant strapped on her back. A drunk man on the sidewalk jumped to his feet, sobered up instantly, and guided her to the other side. Then he sat back down and returned to being drunk. And from my experience, that's what most people are like—not drunk, but ready and willing to help.

Because my blindness was less severe than some of the other kids at the School, I got used to leading others, contrary to the way I was in public school. All that to say that no matter what I did after graduation, I preferred leading the way rather than following along.

While at Saint Mary's, I got my first taste of leadership on a much larger scale than leading line-ups at the School for the Blind. I applied for and got a grant from the Federal Government to provide summer employment to blind students in Halifax. I managed that project with Chris Stark, the same Chris from the School who brought us apples from the Valley every year. Some of the students did research that summer on other schools for the blind, different methods for teaching, unemployment data, or review of laws having anything to do with blind people. We also lobbied vigorously that summer for the most basic of rights on behalf of blind people. When a few years later I thought I might want to be a lawyer, it probably had something to do with the kind of work we were doing that summer.

Toward the end of the summer project, the phone rang and it was the office of Bob Stanfield, then Leader of the Opposition in Ottawa. He was on his way home to Halifax for the weekend and wanted to follow up on some of the many letters we'd written to him and anyone else who could read. We wrote about everything from the need for Braille and large-print textbooks to access to jobs. It may have been the early 1970s, but there was no end of outstanding issues needing attention, despite the work of the CNIB.

We showed up on Saturday morning, Chris and I and some other blind students on the project, respectfully dressed in suits and ties. Mr. Stanfield wore blue jeans and a white T-shirt. We talked and he listened. At the end of the meeting, he told us to keep writing letters and not to take "no" for an answer. Coming from him, in that deep-toned Stanfield voice, it was all the encouragement we needed.

Law School was not as daunting as I thought it would be, but I had to be there to see for myself that it wasn't really my cup of tea. I didn't like the straight-line, logical thinking or the rigors of trying to find a precedent in a haystack of big books with tiny print.

CHAPTER TWENTY

Blindness aside, I was born under a cluster of lucky stars that followed me from the day my parents brought me to the School in Halifax, to right now, retired and teaching myself to write, by just writing. In between then and now I raised a family while living and working for a time in Halifax, Regina, Vancouver, Toronto, Ottawa, and now Charlottetown where, under one of those lucky stars, I got to retire.

It wasn't a planned journey or an obsession to live only in capital cities; it's just the way it happened. Along the way I found myself in the midst of one exciting endeavour after another, in places made for dreams. I'll mention a few of them, but for no other reason than to show what potential there is in everyone when doors are opened.

By age thirty, I was sitting behind a desk at the CNIB headquarters in Toronto, just appointed President and Chief Executive Officer for the CNIB, with 65,000 blind and visually impaired clients, 3,000 staff, 100,000 volunteers, and a multi-million-dollar catering business to manage. I recall more than once looking out at the six lanes of traffic on Bayview Avenue and wondering how I had gotten there, all the way from failing Grade Three.

Of course, you don't rise to the top without a lot of hard work along the way, but more than that, I made the grade because I was full of confidence and youthful idealism, enough to turn heads. I got that confidence at the School for the Blind in Halifax and the youthful idealism, that was just my age.

On the day the Constitution was repatriated in Ottawa, I was there on Parliament Hill, with two pre-school blind children, to present the Prime Minister, The Honourable Pierre Trudeau, with a leather-embossed, Braille copy of the new Constitution.

When the Prime Minister entered the room, he made a beeline for the two kids. In his best suit, he sat on the floor and talked to them about his busy morning with the Queen. The little girl asked him if the Queen had two heads, a fairy tale, I suppose, and with the loud laughter that followed, I didn't hear the answer.

It rained heavily that morning. I was assigned a seat up front for the repatriation ceremony alongside Bob Stanfield. I thanked him for telling us in

Halifax, way back then, not to take "no" for an answer: simple advice but advice that served me well over the years.

On a few occasions, I was in Wayne Gretzky's home in Brantford, Ontario, sitting at the kitchen table with his father and mother. The Annual Wayne Gretzky Tennis Tournaments that followed those discussions raised millions for the work of the CNIB. I got to meet and have a drink with "The Great One" and too many Hall of Famers to mention. I didn't see that in the stars when huddled around the television at the School in Halifax, waiting for the puck to drop.

As proud as I was to serve as President of the Institute, I needed a change after three years of living out of a suitcase. At half the salary and few perks by comparison, I embarked on a second career, this time in the federal public service, beginning at the Treasury Board in Ottawa with a staff of six instead of thousands, and a much smaller office. But I got to be home for most evenings and weekends. It took me at least six months to understand the language and work culture of the public service.

Eventually, I moved on to teaching leadership to senior public servants at the Canadian Centre for Management Development. Teaching without notes was not easy in the beginning, but all the practice at the School for the Blind, doing mathematics in my head and creating mental prompts, served me well. I signed up as a member of the faculty for one year and stayed for six.

Ten years later, I was standing proudly on the steps of the Canadian National Vimy Memorial in northern France. I had been there many times before in my new role as Assistant Deputy Minister at Veterans Affairs Canada, but this time it was extra special. It was the 90th Anniversary of the Battle of Vimy Ridge and I was there, in charge of the events, and leading a large delegation of veterans, veterans' organizations, students, parliamentarians, and dignitaries.

I took a deep breath as the Minister and a host of other delegates mounted the stairs of the Memorial for a closer look at the ribbon of names so meticulously chiselled in the stone walls surrounding the Monument: the names of 11,168 Canadian soldiers with no known grave, killed or presumed dead during the First World War.

It was the day before the ceremonies and I was too busy on that occasion to fully appreciate the walkabout. But so far, whether arrangements for Her Majesty the Queen or the President of France, all was going well. There were no phone calls from the Prime Minister's officer and that was better than good news. Airplanes and helicopters were busy overhead, scanning the property to make sure all was safe and secure.

I was a bit nervous as well, considering the importance of what was to unfold the next day. It had been a full two years of preparation and more than a few challenges along the way, but I knew we were ready and the weather for the next day said so as well: a sunny 23 degrees Celsius, in stark contrast to the awful cold and snow that faced the soldiers on the actual days of the battle in 1917.

And to see as many as 5,000 Canadian students in attendance from schools across the country, and the young children from the Confederation Centre Charlottetown Youth Chorus, there performing the signature piece, "I'm Dreaming of Home:" that was something you never forget.

Weeks earlier, I had lunch with the Queen's Private Secretary in preparation for Her Majesty's role at Vimy, and I wasn't about to miss telling him of the just-in-case dinner my mother made for the Queen, back in 1957, in case her car broke down in front of the house. He was even interested to know what she had cooked and he told me he'd share that story with the Queen—and, if he did, I hope my mother was listening.

I was privileged as well to lead a delegation of Aboriginal Veterans, Elders, native students, the Governor General, and other dignitaries on a ten-day pilgrimage to Europe, to bring home the spirits of their fallen soldiers. The ceremonies and events in traditional dress and drums were breathtaking and unforgettable.

And yet another star overhead saw me in northern France as part of the Canadian delegation to unearth the remains of an unknown soldier, now entombed at the National War Memorial in Ottawa.

Of course, I never got to play baseball for the Baltimore Orioles, as I thought possible in Grade Five, but I did get to umpire a few Little League baseball games. And I did okay at it, except once, when I called out "ball four" and the catcher, all of eleven years old, jumped up and shouted, "Mister, are you blind? He swung at the ball!" I left it at that—"ball four," that is—and sent the batter to first base anyway.

Little wrinkles like that are just part of being visually impaired and I've had my share over the years: talking to a sweater, thinking it was the cat; getting on the wrong bus or off at the wrong stop, a lot more than once; or stopping to ask a mannequin for directions. It's just part of the package: embarrassing when younger, and, when older, fodder for a good laugh.

Today I write books, some that get read and some not. And overall, I'd admit that being visually impaired is a real nuisance at times, but it's nothing to what it would have been if I had stayed home instead of going to the School in Halifax. As a result, I pretty well got to do what everyone else did, and then some.

EPILOGUE

I'm told the sun was shining the day the wrecking crew turned on the old School and struck it down in 1984. Supervisor, Cleon Smith, was there and Steve, too, the school carpenter—the same Steve who cut my hair for nine years. Cleon told me recently how sad a day it was for both of them as the walls caved in.

Back in the early 1970s, a group of former students from the School, me included, lobbied vigorously for a new school for the blind. The hundred-year-old building was no longer a safe place for housing children, blind or otherwise. Someone needed to say so and, unfortunately, a lot more than that got said when the media latched onto the story.

We proposed a new but smaller school, less of a residence and more of a resource centre to support blind students attending local schools, including support for their teachers and parents. Integration of the sort, for people with disabilities, was happening around the world, and we thought it time to do likewise. That's what we brought to the Government, but with not much said in return, we turned to the press.

Unfortunately, the media took over and for the better part of a year, newspaper headlines with words like "barbaric" and "neglectful" gave a very false impression of the old School, at least the School I had attended. But there was no halting the runaway train. There was no intent, on our part at least, ever to suggest that staff and teachers at the School were not doing their level best for the kids. But the message for change that we tried to deliver was nowhere near as eye-catching as what appeared in the headlines.

The Government of Nova Scotia was not happy with me or with some of the other blind people who were lobbying publicly for a new School for the Blind. And, for that, they stopped the financial support I needed to continue my studies at Law School. As I write it now, I'm again as shocked as I was back then, upon hearing it for the first time.

It was an official from the department of Welfare who called me with the bad news. He was forthright in pointing out that issues of blindness, and the School, in particular, were politically charged, damaging to the ruling Party. I couldn't wait to get off the phone and head down to the Premier's office.

I knew the Premier, Gerald Regan, from one meeting and another and I was certain he'd fix it. Long story short, he didn't, and although I could have raised a few eyebrows in the media, I was a bit fearful of closing too many doors before even starting a career. I was married by then and took the bad news as good reason to leave Law School and find a job.

After the dark clouds had dissipated and cooler heads prevailed, a new facility was built, a few blocks from the former site. The residential model for education of blind children had given way to integration. Blind children remained at home with their families and at schools with kids from their own neighbourhood.

Home is where they belong, like other kids, as long as local schools, teachers, and legislators continue to take care and go the extra mile. And as they do, there's a wealth of experience to draw upon, thanks to the ground-breaking work and lessons learned at the Halifax School for the Blind.

The School property is now a parking lot for the VG Hospital, but every time I'm there I feel the same sense of loss as I did when they tore down the house that Dad built in the country. It's as if the School was still there and you could just walk in and there'd be the old crowd.

And if I could, I'd head for the boys' room downstairs for a game of poker-pool with Gary, an episode of *Star Trek* with Martin Collicutt, a walk along the iron fence around the schoolyard when the lilacs are in full bloom, or, better still, I'd spend an afternoon in Grade Eleven with the same teachers and the same group that graduated in 1967.

In 2012, as a final tribute to the old School and the good memories left in its wake, former students commissioned the design and building of a fitting Memorial. We did it ourselves, without government support: the way most of us lived, worked, and volunteered. The Memorial now stands on University Avenue where the School once did: a proud reminder of good times and victories won.

I travelled to Halifax from Charlottetown to attend the unveiling ceremony, accompanied by my wife, Susan, and a life-long friend from the School, Vivian MacLean. At the ceremony, we were joined by dignitaries, former staff, and close friends of the School. In all that was said that morning, one thing was abundantly clear: the old School was a good friend to most of us who had studied there and to those who helped us along the way.

Embedded within the Braille dots and the beautifully embossed image of the School building on the face of the Monument are the lives of thousands, and no end of valuable lessons learned over 113 years.

A totally blind friend of mine, and former student at the School, Jean McAllister, said it poignantly in a tribute song she wrote and sang for the occasion. It meant enough for her to travel all the way from Orillia, Ontario, to be there. While she sang, I felt as I had when there, enjoying the classroom, the other kids, and missing home at the same time. The chorus that follows says it better than words alone:

There were pillow fights and singing nights
And nights we cried ourselves to sleep.
There were friendships and loves with
bonds that grew as strong as steel
Our home away from home,
its memories ours to keep.
And I've often wondered, through the years,
how did our mothers feel?

I know how *my* mother felt. As good as the School was for me, she never stopped asking me if she had done the right thing. I never stopped telling her "yes," but still she wondered about it until she died.

After the Memorial ceremony, we were graciously hosted for lunch at the site of a new umbrella organization, the Atlantic Provinces Special Education Authority (APSEA). It was no longer a "school" for the blind, but rather a resource centre dedicated to providing support to blind and also deaf students now attending local schools in their own communities.

There are times when students may travel to the centre in Halifax for a short period of time (often one week) to obtain intensive training in a particular skill area such as Braille or mobility training, but, for the most part, the support they receive is based in the neighbourhood school setting.

I could see right away that everything had changed, and as much as the old School was right for its time, so is this one for today, a resource centre, more like the one we had lobbied for some years earlier.

We had a reception/reunion at the hotel that evening, and for me and everyone there it was like being back at the School. We saw each other as we were when we were children back in the day, but with adult voices, grown-up thoughts, and a lot more to say. The words, "Do you remember when," began one story after another and it was just as much fun being there as it would have been for any family together again after fifty years apart.

That gathering as well, like the embossed image of the School on the Memorial, was a fitting tribute to those who built the School in the first place. In the room that evening, behind the smiles and the stories, were professional musicians, physiotherapists, legal secretaries, teachers, piano tuners, computer programmers, canteen operators, business owners, public servants, counsellors, mothers, fathers, and grandparents, all blind and all former students of the old School.

In making the rounds I overheard someone mention having talked that day to Mr. Nickerson, one of my favourite teachers who, by then, was in his nineties and to my surprise living just up the street from the hotel. I got his phone number and called that very evening. We met the next morning and, now and again, before he passed away, we continued to meet. He, too, had fond memories of the School, complete with details of things I had long since forgotten.

Sir Frederick Fraser, the first Superintendent of the School, would have been as proud that evening as he was when knighted by King George V for his life-long attention to the education and general well-being of blind people in Atlantic Canada and beyond.

He'd be proud, too, I'm sure, if you stopped by to visit the School Memorial on University Avenue. And if you do, take a few moments and feel the embossed image of the School and the Braille lettering on the face of the Monument. Then close your eyes and listen carefully: you might just hear the sound of a brass bell, waking the kids for another day at school.

APPENDIX

WHAT THE KIDS WERE SAYING

At various intervals, the students at the Halifax School for the Blind published their own newspaper, funded mostly from sales within the School and a few advertisements from outside. Following are just some of the student/staff articles that appeared in the early 1960s and a few that date back to the mid 1950s. They appear pretty much as written back in the day, although a few have been shortened or edited where words were too faded to read.

KINDERGARTEN TO GRADE THREE

I used to worry when I came to school. I worried whether my mother would forget to come or she wouldn't be able to find me...

(Maria Ritchie)

I felt so sick when I first came to the school but my mother kept saying it was a wonderful place. Now I think it's okay, I guess. My mother phones me and comes to see me so the time goes pretty fast.

(Robby Ganong)

I used to go to school at home but it wasn't nice at all. I was glad when Daddy brought me here. Nancy, Claudine and I do a lot of things together.

(Cathy Buckland)

I was afraid of this place when I came. I was afraid some of the boys would beat me up. Now I have friends. I've got lots of boys to play with.

(Danny Harnish)

I am a totally blind student at the School here in Halifax and I laugh when somebody thinks blind students can't do things that other boys and girls can do. I can bounce, catch and recite the pieces that go along with bouncing the ball as good as anyone in the younger fry class. I bounce the ball from one to one-hundred and I know also a chum of mine in the School by the name of Roy Green who can climb better than any student in the school, and he also knows when the supervisor is around. James Noseworthy who is also totally blind can run as fast as any of us and can sing and play the piano quite well... While mischief is afoot, let a supervisor appear and who ducks first? You guessed it, the boys with no vision.

(Brian Vey)

I have a pussy willows tree that
grows outside our house
And one day, sitting on a branch
was a little grey mouse.
He jumped down to the ground,
as fearless as could be
Maybe he was afraid to stay
Or maybe, afraid of me.

(Anne Masterton)

Lawrence Cacopardo, Joe, to all the students at the school is our night watchman. He is very kind to all of us, especially kind to the smaller boys and girls, and when he comes around at night to make sure we are all safe, he always jokes with us. Many a dark night we feel better when we see uncle Joe as we call him.

(Kenny Church)

Misses Helen Corbett and Claudine Chiasson took on Mr. Hawes in a game of Old Maid over the Easter vacation and we hear that Mr. Hawes lost. Hope you didn't cheat, girls.

(Miss Ruth Connors, Junior Supervisor)

Once I came for a visit when I was four, then my daddy brought me to stay. I cried because I was lonesome. Now I never cry because I have too much fun.

(Wayne Hounsell, Kindergarten)

There is a little boy,
Who has a little cat,
He has a little toy train,
And a ball and bat.
There is a little bird,
Up in the tree,
It always stops,
And sings for me.

(Barbara LeGay)

...I am going on a train trip this summer and so is my friend. We will have a feast on pink peppermints.

(Paul English)

...When it became too wet outdoors, we went down to the playroom. The four three-wheelers and the three wagons made lots of noise. At bedtime Robby lost another tooth. He put it under his pillow but it was still there in the morning. Then early Monday, a parcel of candy and treats arrived from his mother. We all enjoyed the red marshmallow hearts and corn twists.

(Juniors' Corner)

We were surprised and delighted when our supervisor Mr. MacNeil told us that he would take the small fry on a walk to Dartmouth across the Halifax bridge. We started out from the school and walked to the bridge, the third largest bridge in the world. There were twenty boys on the walk... Jimmie and Dermott O'Keefe as well as Donald Harnish and Wayne Huskins were holding on to Mr. MacNeil's coattails, badly frightened by the height of the bridge.

(Kenny Church)

GRADES FOUR TO EIGHT

I am twelve years of age and my home is in Fredericton. I must confess that I did not know what to expect when I told daddy that I would attend the School for the Blind in Halifax. My fears soon came to an end when Daddy took me to the School and I was introduced to the Superintendent, Mr. Hawes, Principal Legge and other members of the staff. I found that the classes were smaller both as to the number of students per class and also the size of the classrooms. I also found that I was behind in some subjects while advanced in others... The manner of teaching was the same except that more time is given to each pupil. I like all my teachers. We have Gym classes twice weekly under Mr. McGarrity and we have swim classes weekly at Stadacona. We have our own outdoor skating rink, bowl three times a week if we care to, and the senior students have their own boys club... In addition, we are given school concerts, parties, treats, etc.... After my stay to date, I think I can honestly say, I hope I will be a student here for years to come.

(Michael Kilburn)

I think I speak for all the younger students in our school when I say we all like morning Assembly because at it we start the day with prayer and songs of praise plus interesting stories, articles from the paper or nice little talks. We finish the day with prayer, bedtime stories and sometimes a funny act or two... Some of the boys and girls like winter because everything is so dark and cold on the outside while we feel snug and warm on the inside. Then, sleep and dreams of Bomba the jungle boy, Robinson Crusoe or the Bobbsey Twins...

(Tommy Anstey)

...let's take a peep at what Easter in the School meant to over half the students (the ones who couldn't get home for Easter) ...thanks to the hard efforts of Mrs. Woodworth and her staff we sat down to a really fine turkey dinner with all the trimmings. Next was the eye opener, strawberry shortcake with whipped cream. Did our mouths water... The small fry ate the poor bunny's eggs and later, we hate to admit, old bunny himself graced the table. Chocolate eggs and bunnies disappeared and contents of boxes from home then disappointed. Outdoor games, walks, bowling, movies, singsongs with the twist added for good measure, took up the students' time. Bridge, Hearts, etc., were played by the older students and all in all, it was a wonderful Easter season. Thanks from us all to all who contributed.

(Emile Haché)

During the year Mr. Allen reads stories at morning Assembly. He reads different kinds of stories such as fairy stories for the younger folk, animal stories and tales of the sea for the oldsters. By listening very carefully we find many of these stories have a moral or two built in.

(Gilbert Murray, 1955)

GRADES NINE TO ELEVEN

...A school paper must have a policy and what better motive could be ours than last year's slogan: "What's good for the school is good for us." In my opinion, such a slogan ties in with our opinion of the school: "There may be Bigger but try and find a Better."

(Cleon Smith, Editor)

Newspaper week began November 19th with the staff of the paper illustrating on stage the duties of the School paper. The feature editor, Gloria Berry, was mistress of ceremonies. The following day there was an exhibition of former school papers... Thursday, the staff of the paper provided and distributed pop and candy to the Junior boys and girls which we were glad to do and they appreciated it very much.

(Alice Higgins and Clara Hawco)

Since two classes were working at the same pace and had the same spelling teacher, a spelling match was arranged. Mr. Allen surprised us by attending the match... One by one the students were omitted from the match until three stood on each side. Then the game was discontinued because of lack of time. The spelling teacher, Mrs. McCluskey, provided delicious homemade fudge which was enjoyed by the whole group.

(Michele Fagan)

There are many items to be considered about food besides the eating of it. In a residential school of our size many people join forces to plan, prepare and serve the food... To show the quantity of food we consume in a month, here are some of the figures: butter - 400 pounds; eggs - 120 dozen; milk - 3,588 quarts; beef - 663 pounds; pork - 125 pounds; bacon - 140 pounds; hot dogs - 204 pounds; cheese - 58 pounds; peanut butter - 42 pounds; potatoes - 60 bags and bread - 1049 loaves, not including the 150 loaves the cook, Mrs. Woodworth, bakes every month.

(Editor, 1962)

The regular piano/organ tuning course at the school takes from four to five years. The student after finishing a five-year course is presented with a tuning certificate. Oliver Cormier is the teacher and is a very popular man with his pupils... Others listed in this year's course are, Messrs. David Baird, Fred Haines and Donald Rowe. A student commencing his course first becomes acquainted with the necessary tools and both the piano and organ. He is then taught the Tuning Hammer Technique. Instructions in repairs start the same time as running. Special text books are used and the teacher lectures as he demonstrates. On the completion of the course a certificate holder is able to tune as well as repair both the piano and the organ. Some tuners are capable of tuning other musical instruments. The piano tuner must have a knowledge of music and plenty of patience...

(LeRoy Murray, piano tuning graduate)

A trace of sadness hangs over the School this year because of the sudden, unexpected death of Mr. O. Cormier. He was our well-loved tuning teacher. Mr. Cormier had been our tuning instructor for some years and he was a man well loved by all... He was a man who never got angry at the students if they made a mistake. He would always say it is by mistakes that we learn... The question in our minds is, what will our next teacher be like. Will he be as good as Mr. Cormier?...

(David Baird)

The embossed print library in this School is the oldest of its kind in Canada. Started as a circulating library in the year 1880, following a donation of thirty dollars... At the end of the year, Superintendent Fraser was able to report donations of 435 dollars and many outstanding pledges... In the year 1887 the Braille system was introduced into the classrooms and 47 volumes in the new Braille were purchased for the library. At the time of its inception our library was intended to supply reading material to the blind of the Maritime provinces. Due to the bulkiness and weight of the Braille volumes, the heavy postage charges almost wrecked the plan... In 1898 Mr. Fraser induced the Postmaster General to introduce a bill to Parliament to allow the privilege of free postage for all embossed reading matter for the blind...

(A. Jimmo and D. Keeping, 1956)

At this time, I am very proud to announce the winner of the poetry contest. The winner of the senior group was Linda Barkhouse, Grade Nine and her entry: "An Ode to Spring"

It is a lovely summer's day,
And flowers are in bloom,
Because it is the month of May
The end of Winter's gloom
The green grass growing on the lawn,
The spring air fresh and sweet,
The birds start singing in the dawn
Spring flowers at your feet...
Lessons to study, tests to write
Minds are working: now we wait
Now soon again that fateful night,
See which ones will "graduate."

Dear Boys, read your comment in one of the school papers about not getting samples of food from the girls' cooking class. Well, the reason for that is this: "The nearest way to a man's heart is through his stomach," and since Mr. Allen doesn't approve of romances here in the school, we did not want to tempt you.

(Mrs. F. Munroe, teacher, Domestic Science, 1962)

On Wednesday, October 17th the girls' club celebrated a sixth birthday by going on a drive to Chester. Cars were kindly donated by Mr. Allen, Mr. Rowlings, Mrs. Muggah and Mrs. Cook. A supper was to be served by the Baptist Ladies Auxiliary. Mrs. Cook's car visited Peggy's Cove, Mrs. Muggah's car did likewise. Mr. Rawlings took his group to visit Mrs. Cook, a former supervisor at the school, while Mr. Allen's car arrived very early in Chester and he let his group explore the town on foot. After a turkey supper in the Church hall, Mary Whiffen, herself totally blind, entertained us with piano selections to the enjoyment of all.

(Jean McAllister)

ACKNOWLEDGEMENTS

No one was more helpful to me in the writing of this book than my wife, Susan Greene. I can't thank her enough for hours upon hours of patience and thoughtful feedback. She was my eyes when I needed to see something I couldn't see.

There'd be no book either, if not for my friend, Harvey Sawler, who encouraged me to write the book in the first place, and a few times after that, too. He even suggested the title for the book. Thank you, Harvey!

A special thank you as well to school friends Cleon Smith, Vivian MacLean, Fred Haines, Gloria Berry, Jean McAllister, Melvin MacNeil, Monte Single, Martin Collicutt and Tommy Anstey for helping to jog my memory.

I was also encouraged by the enthusiastic way my brothers and sisters responded to an early draft of the book.

The editor, Ann Thurlow, was most thoughtful and helpful, from the first sentence of the Author's Preface to the last line of the Epilogue. Thank you, Ann!

I'm grateful as well to Acorn Press, and particularly Terrilee Bulger, for liking the book well enough to publish it.

And finally, if she doesn't mind, I'd like to say another "thank you" to my wife, Susan; she does *that* much for me and my books, one day to the next.

ABOUT THE AUTHOR

Robert Mercer grew up in Sydney, Nova Scotia, and spent nine years in Halifax, at the residential School for the Blind.

Robert has self-published *Abigail in the Land of Green Gables*, a poem-story for children, and three Kindle eBooks: *Biography Bites* in two volumes and *Consciousness, You and the Caterpillar*, a layman's look at life and death. He draws on his own experiences as someone with a visual impairment, from his time at school, and from a lifetime of service in the voluntary sector and the federal public service.

He lives in Charlottetown.

robertfmercer@yahoo.com